Your Friend, The Holy Spirit

Your Friend, The Holy Spirit

Morris L. Venden

Pacific Press Publishing Association
Boise, Idaho
Montemorelos, Nuevo Leon, Mexico
Oshawa, Ontario, Canada

Edited by Don Mansell
Designed by Tim Larson
Cover Illustration by Eric Joyner
Type set in 10/12 Century Schoolbook

Copyright © 1986 by
Pacific Press Publishing Association
Printed in United States of America
All Rights Reserved

Library of Congress Cataloging in Publication Data

Venden, Morris L.
  Your friend, the Holy Spirit.

  1. Holy Spirit. 2. Seventh-day Adventists—Doctrines. I. Title.
BT121.2.V36   1986   231'.3   86-25170
ISBN 0-8163-0682-6

Contents

1. Your Friend, the Holy Spirit — 7
2. The Work of the Holy Spirit — 15
3. The Holy Spirit and Conviction — 21
4. The Holy Spirit and Conversion — 27
5. The Holy Spirit and Cleansing — 35
6. The Crisis of Surrender — 47
7. The Holy Spirit and the Commission for Service — 53
8. How to Receive the Baptism of the Holy Spirit — 61
9. The Search for the Spectacular — 69
10. The Gift of Tongues — 79
11. The Fourth Angel's Message — 87

Chapter 1
Your Friend, the Holy Spirit

What do you think of when you think of the Holy Spirit? Do you picture the Holy Ghost as a mysterious and perhaps somewhat spooky phantom? Do you consider the Holy Spirit just an influence, or power, instead of a real person? Have you ever thought of the Holy Spirit as being very touchy, easily insulted and grieved? Or do you recognize the Holy Spirit as one of the best Friends you could ever have?

We often refer to the Holy Spirit as an "It." Sometimes we talk about our need to get more of "It." But if the Holy Spirit were simply an "It," we could approach the Holy Spirit as the heathen do their witch doctors or idols. We might think that if we could get more of "It," we would have reason for pride, for we would be in control of a mighty power, becoming some sort of spiritual supermen. But on the other hand, if the Holy Spirit is a person, then instead of His being a power that we use, He is the One who uses us, to the glory of God. Instead of trying to get more of the Holy Spirit, we become interested in His getting more of us. Do you see the difference? There are many Christians today who are trying to use the Holy Spirit.

One time a friend of mine invited me to a meeting of a charismatic group in a large hotel in Los Angeles. One of the speakers at this prayer breakfast was almost commanding the Holy Spirit, or at least that's what it sounded like to some of us. "Speaking in tongues," he said, "there's nothing to speaking in tongues! I can speak in tongues any time I want to." And he broke into tongues. But the Bible teaching is that it is the Holy

Spirit who gives the gift of tongues, and that's why it sounded like this man was controlling the Holy Spirit instead of the Spirit controlling him. One might question which spirit was involved!

The Bible teaches that the Holy Spirit is a separate Being. He is not simply an influence, an extension of the other members of the Godhead, such as the spirit of God or the spirit of Christ. Instead, He is the third Person of the Godhead, a separate person who is as fully God as God the Father and God the Son. At the baptism of Jesus, the Holy Ghost descended in a bodily shape like a dove. See Luke 3:21, 22. The gospel commission, in Matthew 28:19, instructs Christ's followers to baptize in the name of the Father, and of the Son, and of the Holy Ghost, or Holy Spirit. Jesus said He would ask His Father to send the Comforter, or Holy Spirit, to abide with His disciples after His ascension. See John 14:16; 16:7. And Jesus also promised that the Spirit would guide them into all truth. See John 16:13. So the Holy Spirit is a member of the Trinity, equal with the Father and the Son.

Those who have studied the matter of personality have come up with several elements which are necessary to make up a person. Even on the human level, we know that personality is not based on physical characteristics, such as having hands and feet. We have all heard of people who were blind or deaf or crippled, but who still had beautiful personalities. Personality is instead made up of at least three basic elements: (1) a mind, the capacity to think, ability to acquire knowledge, and the ability to reason, (2) feelings and emotions, and (3) the power of decision or choice—the will.

For a Bible example of the first trait, let's look at 1 Corinthians 2:10, 11. It says that God has revealed certain things to us by His Spirit, and then it says, "The Spirit searcheth all things, yea, the deep things of God." Have you ever been interested in the possibility of searching into the deep things of God? The Holy Spirit is interested in that, too, and yet the Holy Spirit *is* God. It must be that the Holy Spirit is searching deeply into the things of the Father and the Son, don't you suppose? Verse 11: "What man knoweth the things of a man, save the spirit of man which is in him? even so the things of God knoweth no man, but the Spirit of God." So here you have the first element of personality: knowing, searching for knowledge.

Another scripture on this same point is found in Nehemiah 9:20, 21. Speaking of God: "Thou gavest also thy good spirit to instruct them, and withheldest not thy manna from their mouth, and gavest them water for their thirst. Yea, forty years didst thou sustain them in the wilderness." So the Spirit is good, and the Spirit instructed the people of Israel. In order to be an instructor or teacher, you have to have knowledge, and personality.

Second, consider the emotions and feelings. Does the Holy Spirit have feelings? A familiar text here would be Ephesians 4:30: "Grieve not the holy Spirit of God, whereby ye are sealed unto the day of redemption." We are admonished not to grieve the Holy Spirit, so the Holy Spirit can be grieved. It is not possible to grieve a power or an influence, but it is possible to grieve a person.

Now this text has sometimes been understood to mean that the Holy Spirit is just waiting for a chance to leave us. How many people have said, "I've gone too far. The Holy Spirit has left me. I'm afraid I've committed the unpardonable sin." No, no, no! The Holy Spirit can be grieved because He is a Person, but He never leaves us. The Holy Spirit never leaves us, although it is possible for us to leave Him.

There is no such thing as the Spirit coming to the point where He says, "I've had enough. I'm fed up with you. You've hurt my feelings. I'm leaving." The Holy Spirit follows us year after year, as long as there is any possibility of a response on our part. He stayed with the people of Israel for centuries, bearing long with their rebellion and their stubborn hearts. It is a very difficult thing to walk away from the Holy Spirit. It is not easily accomplished.

Why is it so difficult to leave the Holy Spirit? Because of His love. Love never knows when it is enough. Love does not give up easily. First Corinthians 13 tells us that love can outlast anything, and is, in fact, the one thing that still stands when all else has fallen. Romans 15:30 speaks of the love of the Holy

Spirit. Have you ever thought about how much the Holy Spirit loves you? We speak of the love of God; we sing of the love of Jesus. But the Holy Spirit loves as well. "Now I beseech you, brethren, for the Lord Jesus Christ's sake, and for the love of the Spirit, that ye strive together with me in your prayers to God for me." Love is also an emotion, and this is yet another evidence of the personality of the Spirit of God. He loves. He loves each one of us with the immeasurable love of God.

And finally, number three, the Holy Spirit has a will, or the power of decision and choice. First Corinthians 12:11, speaking of the gifts of the Spirit, says, "All these worketh that one and the selfsame Spirit, dividing to every man severally as he will." Notice, as He will. The Holy Spirit has a will, or the power of choice.

Another type of evidence of the personality of the Holy Spirit is His work, or actions as a person. He accomplishes things that a mere influence could not accomplish. As we have already noticed, He searches the deep things of God. See 1 Corinthians 2:10. Romans 8:26 speaks of the Spirit praying. "Likewise the Spirit also helpeth our infirmities: for we know not what we should pray for as we ought: but the Spirit itself maketh intercession for us with groanings which cannot be uttered." The Spirit prays for us and helps our infirmities. Sounds like a person, doesn't it? And if a person is praying for you, interceding for you, then He's on your side, He's your Friend.

Hebrews 7:25 tells us that Jesus is also an intercessor for us, and with both Jesus and the Holy Spirit praying for us and interceding for us, how can we lose? It must take a great deal of stubbornness for anyone to be lost with those kinds of forces on our side.

What is it that causes a person to lose out on redemption? It is his determined resistance against the mighty forces of heaven. I don't want to resist them, do you? I want the prayers of the Holy Spirit, and the prayers of Jesus, to be answered for me.

Revelation speaks repeatedly of the Spirit having a message for the churches. Revelation 2:7 is an example. "He that hath an ear, let him hear what the Spirit saith unto the churches."

The Holy Spirit communicates to God's church, once again an evidence of personality.

John 15:26 tells us that the Holy Spirit is a witness. A witness has to be more than just an influence! When you picture a court scene, you must have witnesses, and witnesses are persons. Jesus says, "When the Comforter is come, whom I will send unto you from the Father, even the Spirit of truth, which proceedeth from the Father, he shall testify of me." In the same discourse, Jesus speaks of the Holy Spirit in another function—that of a Teacher. "The Comforter, which is the Holy Ghost, whom the Father will send in my name, he shall teach you all things." John 14:26. Jesus took courage from the fact that the Holy Spirit could teach His disciples things that even Jesus couldn't say at that time, and also, that the Spirit would bring to their memory the things Jesus had tried to teach them when He was with them. See John 16:12-14.

Another activity of the Holy Spirit is found in Acts 16:6, 7. It is an indication of the authority of the Holy Spirit. "When they had gone throughout Phrygia and the region of Galatia, and were forbidden of the Holy Ghost to preach the word in Asia, after they were come to Mysia, they assayed to go into Bithynia: but the Spirit suffered them not." So the Holy Spirit was in command of the work, guiding and directing the early Christian church.

In Acts 13:2, it says, "As they ministered to the Lord, and fasted, the Holy Ghost said, Separate me Barnabas and Saul for the work whereunto I have called them." Looking at this text how can anyone miss the reality that the Holy Spirit is a person, One with supreme authority in God's church? This point is also mentioned in Acts 20:28, "Take heed therefore unto yourselves, and unto all the flock, over the which the Holy Ghost hath made you overseers, to feed the church of God, which he hath purchased with his own blood."

We could go on and on presenting evidence that the Holy Spirit is a person. In Isaiah 63:10, for instance, you find that we can vex Him. In Hebrews 10:29 we are told of those who have done despite to the Spirit. Acts 5:3 speaks of lying to the Spirit, and in Matthew 12:31, 32, it warns about speaking against

Him. But the greatest news about the personality of the Holy Spirit is found in John 14:16, 17. The Holy Spirit, the Comforter, is come to abide with us, to dwell with us and in us. What a comfort to know that one of the mighty Persons of the Godhead has come to dwell with us. See *The Desire of Ages,* page 671. He is everywhere present. And He comes in His power and love to dwell with us during our stay here on this earth.

Have you ever wished you could have lived when Christ was here on earth, when God Himself was present among men? That would be a wonderful experience. But today we have available to us the privilege of living on the earth at a time when another Person of the Godhead is dwelling among us—the Holy Spirit. And since the Holy Spirit is not hampered by the limitations of humanity, He can be everywhere present, close to you, to me, to every person on the face of the earth. And He is with us every moment of every day, unless we deliberately leave Him and refuse His company.

We can have a theological acceptance of the Holy Spirit as a Person, but what could be more important than to have an experiential acceptance of Him as a Friend? He is one of the best Friends any of us could ever have. He stands beside us; He is the Comforter in all the circumstances of life.

Have you ever felt the need for a Comforter? I can remember going off to college and getting bogged down studying for exams. One day I woke up and said to my brother, who was my roommate, "I wish I could go to bed and sleep for a week."

That day I was up on the athletic field, pole vaulting, and the pole broke. I landed on my head, knocked myself out, and got a brain concussion. The doctor said, "Go to bed for a week."

My folks heard about it. They were 500 miles away, but faster than I thought possible, they were there by my bedside to bring comfort.

That's the way it is with the Holy Spirit. The Holy Spirit is always by our side, always there. When you went through the struggle to give up on yourself and come to Jesus for the first time, He was there. As you meet the discouragements and trials of daily life, He is there. When the enemy comes in like a flood, He is there to lift up a standard against the enemy for you. When you've tried to fight your own battles and ended up bruised and bleeding and thought God could not forgive you, the Holy Spirit was there, to reassure you of the Father's love and of the ability of Jesus to save unto the uttermost all who come unto God by Him.

The Holy Spirit is by your side. He's your Friend. Do you believe it? He's a real Person, and He is your Friend today. How fitting the words to the familiar song of praise, "Glory be to the Father, and to the Son, and to the Holy Ghost." He deserves our praise, our love, and our gratitude as we accept His friendship and care.

Chapter 2
The Work of the Holy Spirit

There was a man in Arizona a number of years ago who was having severe problems. He had been a Seventh-day Adventist, but he had backslidden and was completely discouraged. He had become an alcoholic and would get drunk, beat his wife and kids, and break up the furniture. He couldn't hold a job and found himself increasingly in financial straits.

One night, completely discouraged, he was walking down the street considering ending it all. As he walked along, he came to a tent where some religious meetings were being held. He wandered into the back of the tent, and before the evening was over, someone placed his hands on him, and he received the baptism of the Holy Spirit and began speaking in tongues, then and there.

In addition to the gift of tongues, he received instant and complete victory over his drinking problem, he quit beating his wife and kids, and experienced a dramatic change in his life.

What would you do with that story? Is there anything about it that makes you nervous? Or are you ready to go out and find the first tent meeting you can locate and see if you can experience the same thing?

We all expect the Holy Spirit to be poured out before the end of time. There are some pretty definite predictions in this regard. But consider the following quotation from the book *Evangelism,* page 701. "The descent of the Holy Spirit upon the church is looked forward to as in the future; but it is the privilege of the church to have it now. Seek for it, pray for it, believe for it. We must have it, and Heaven is waiting to bestow it."

There's another one by Ellen White in the *Review and Her-*

ald of November 15, 1892. "It is all-essential for the Christian to understand the meaning of the promise of the holy Spirit just prior to the coming of our Lord Jesus the second time. Talk of it, pray for it, preach concerning it."

There's no doubt about the need for the Holy Spirit in God's church and in our lives today. But we've also been warned that there will be counterfeits—counterfeits so closely resembling the true as to deceive, if possible, the very elect. See Matthew 24:24. How can we distinguish the false from the true manifestation of the Spirit of God?

Perhaps one of the first steps to avoid being deceived in this regard is to remember not to believe everything you hear! It's not safe. Don't believe anything unless you check it out for yourself in the light of the Bible and are satisfied that it agrees. There is value in sharing our ideas and understandings of truth. Sure there is. But the real value should be in the fact that it sparks our interest and moves us to investigate for ourselves. We should never accept what someone says is truth, simply on the basis of that person's say-so.

So the first step in deciding whether or not the experience of the man from Arizona was from the Lord is to *not* take someone's word or even someone's personal experience as being of gospel truth without carefully examining that word or experience in the light of what God's Word teaches in regard to the work of the Holy Spirit.

Going even further: This is the only safe course to pursue in determining whether or not your *own* experiences are of divine origin. We should never judge whether or not something is true simply on the basis of experience. Rather, we should judge our experiences on the basis of the truth of God's Word.

The Word of God was written for two purposes: (1) for information and (2) for communication. It is not enough to have an intellectual understanding of the information given in the Bible. It is equally important for us to have a personal relationship with Jesus Christ, to have communication with Him through His Word and through prayer, so that He can flash His signals to us personally. This two-fold protection is the only safeguard against being deceived.

THE WORK OF THE HOLY SPIRIT 17

With that in mind, I would like to invite you to careful study of the work of the Holy Spirit. I would also like to invite you to continue your one-to-one fellowship with Jesus day by day, as you seek to understand the truths concerning the times we face in the closing scenes of the great controversy.

What can we learn about the genuine work of the Holy Spirit that will give us some clues as to how to recognize the devil's counterfeits? What is the work of the Holy Spirit in the life of the Christian? What is the work of the Holy Spirit in the life of the sinner? Is there a difference?

I'd like to suggest on the basis of my own study that there are four distinct works of the Holy Spirit in the salvation of mankind. We will introduce each of these briefly at this time and then examine each one in depth in the following chapters.

1. *The Holy Spirit's work is to convict the world of sin.* John 16:8 talks about this work of the Holy Spirit. His work includes the whole world. Nobody is left out. Through the Holy Spirit, Jesus, who is the Light of the world, shines on everyone born in this world. John 1:9.

2. *The Holy Spirit's work is to convert the sinner.* John 3:3-5. Jesus said to Nicodemus, "Except a man be born of water and of the Spirit, he cannot enter into the kingdom of God." Another passage on the same point, Titus 3:3-5. "We ourselves also were sometimes foolish, disobedient, deceived, serving divers lusts and pleasures, living in malice and envy, hateful, and hating one another. But after that the kindness and love of God our Saviour toward man appeared, not by works of righteousness which we have done, but according to his mercy he saved us, by the washing of regeneration, and renewing of the Holy Ghost." So the Holy Ghost is involved in regeneration or conversion or the new birth. Romans 12:2 says that He does this by the renewing of our minds.

3. *The Holy Spirit's work is to cleanse the Christian.* First John 1:9 says that if we confess our sins, He is faithful and just to forgive us our sins, and to what?—to *cleanse* us from all unrighteousness. It is through the Holy Spirit that this happens. Notice Ephesians 3:16-19 on this point. "That he would grant you, according to the riches of his glory, to be strengthened

with might by his Spirit in the inner man; that Christ may dwell in your hearts by faith; that ye, being rooted and grounded in love, may be able to comprehend . . . the breadth, and length, and depth, and height; to know the love of Christ." So the person who is experiencing this third work of the Spirit is strengthened with might in the inner person, as Christ dwells in his heart through faith. We have already noticed in John 14 that Christ dwells with us and in us through His Spirit, who was sent to take His place here on earth.

First Corinthians 3:16 and 6:19 speak of our bodies being the temple of the Holy Spirit. This is where He dwells and carries forward His work of cleansing the Christian. The work of cleansing begins at conversion, but a new heart is not necessarily a cleansed heart. Perhaps this inspired comment will help: "Sin could be resisted and overcome only through the mighty agency of the Third Person of the Godhead, who would come with no modified energy, but in the fullness of divine power. It is the Spirit that makes effectual what has been wrought out by the world's Redeemer. It is by the Spirit that the heart is made pure. Through the Spirit the believer becomes a partaker of the divine nature. Christ has given His Spirit as a divine power to overcome all hereditary and cultivated tendencies to evil."—*The Desire of Ages,* page 671. So the third work of the Holy Spirit is to cleanse the heart of the Christian by His indwelling, a process begun at conversion.

4. *The Holy Spirit's work is to commission, or empower the believer for service.* "Ye shall receive power, after that the Holy Ghost is come upon you: and ye shall be witnesses unto me both in Jerusalem, and in all Judaea, and in Samaria, and unto the uttermost part of the earth." Acts 1:8. The fourth work of the Holy Spirit is to bring power for witness, power for sharing the gospel of salvation.

It is important to notice that there is a sequence in the work of the Holy Spirit. It may not be clearly defined where one ends and another begins, but there is a sequence nonetheless. A person will never be converted unless he is first convicted of sin. A person will never be cleansed of sin without the new birth. And a person cannot expect the final work of the Spirit—the baptism of the Spirit, the empowering and commissioning for service—unless he has first been cleansed. Therefore, it is dangerous for any person to look for the baptism of the Holy Spirit, and all of His gifts and spiritual manifestations in the realm of the supernatural, unless he has first received the new birth and the cleansed life.

If one falls into the trap of looking for a shortcut in this process through the spectacular, he may find that the devil will simply replace one form of control for another, one error for another, and the last state of that man will be worse than the first. *Testimonies to Ministers,* page 507, declares: "It was by the confession and forsaking of sin, by earnest prayer and consecration of themselves to God, that the early disciples prepared for the outpouring of the Holy Spirit on the Day of Pentecost. The same work, only in greater degree, must be done now."

The tragedy of Laodicea is that so many have experienced only the first work of the Holy Spirit, or perhaps the first and second. They know they are sinners. They have been convicted of judgment to come. They may have even at one time surrendered themselves to God and experienced the new birth. But they stopped right there and have never continued seeking and praying and desiring the deeper spiritual life.

Here is one more statement on the Holy Spirit's work in our lives: "Christ has promised the gift of the Holy Spirit to His church, and the promise belongs to us as much as to the first disciples. But like every other promise, it is given on conditions. There are many who believe and profess to claim the Lord's promise; they talk *about* Christ and *about* the Holy Spirit, yet receive no benefit. They do not surrender the soul to be guided and controlled by the divine agencies. We can not use the Holy Spirit. The Spirit is to use us. Through the Spirit God works in His people 'to will and to do of His good pleasure.'. . . But many will not submit to this. They want to manage themselves. This is why they do not receive the heavenly gift. Only to those who wait humbly upon God, who watch for His guidance and grace, is the Spirit given. The power of God awaits their demand and reception. This promised blessing, claimed by faith, brings all other blessings in its train."—*The Desire of Ages,* p. 672.

If you have clearly in mind the different phases of the Holy Spirit's work, you have tools with which to face the supposed great manifestations of the Spirit's power in the world today. But never forget that it takes more than information. We must also have the experience of the Holy Spirit in our lives as well, guiding us into all truth. Let's not look at it simply as a theory, thinking that, if we could get all of the Spirit's workings mapped out, we'll be safe. No, we must experience His work in its fullness for ourselves. But this gift from the Father is available to each of us as we pray for it, seek for it, and continue to seek to know Jesus.

Chapter 3
The Holy Spirit and Conviction

Campus Crusade for Christ set a goal a few years ago to reach every home with the gospel by 1980. The method by which they planned to accomplish this was to use the booklet outlining the four spiritual laws. They suggested going down the street, knocking on doors, and trying to get the person who answered the door to go over the four spiritual laws, and then pray, inviting Christ into his life.

Our own church picked up on that goal and encouraged our church members around the world to try to reach every home with the gospel by 1980. During that time, my family was living near Pacific Union College, in a little town in the northern California mountains. It was an Adventist ghetto if I ever saw one. The membership of the church there was around 2,500 people—and the number of non-Adventist families in the entire town turned out to be 40!

Things looked pretty encouraging, there at PUC, for being able to reach the goal in our part of the world. But during that time it was my privilege to visit Bombay, India. One Sabbath evening I met with the handful of believers in Bombay—a city with a population of 8 million people. The church there was not nearly so optimistic. About all they could do in response to the goal set by the General Conference was to wring their hands. They were faced with an impossible task.

But just suppose that we had been able to reach that goal for 1980 this present year. Suppose we had been able to place a tract or a Bible in every home in the world—or even suppose we had been able to visit each home personally for a few minutes and present the four spiritual laws or their equivalent and pray together. Would that mean the work was finished? If I can get a person to pray with me on his doorstep, repeating the words I tell him to say, does that mean he has been reached for Christ? And even if we were able to present Christ on that scale, what would it then take to follow through and present the message of the three angels?

There is only one way that an entire world can be reached—and not only reached with information, but reached with conviction that will make the need for the information evident, and that is through the power of the Holy Spirit. It is the Holy Spirit who one day sent Philip out to the middle of the desert for a divine appointment with a man who was at that moment receptive to the message of Jesus Christ. See Acts 8. It is the Holy Spirit who gave Saul's street address to Ananias, after Saul's experience on the Damascus Road. See Acts 9. It is the Holy Spirit who forbade the gospel to be preached in Asia! Apparently He saw that the time for the gospel to be received in Asia had not yet come. See Acts 16.

On the other hand, we can talk about the Holy Spirit and how it is His work to convict the world of sin, and we can sit back and do nothing and wait for Him do His work. If this is the course we choose, we will miss out on the high privilege of being workers together with God, of sharing with Him in the joy of saving souls.

God's plan is for the Holy Spirit to work through people to reach people. In John 16:7, Jesus told His disciples that He was sending them the Comforter. Notice His words, "I will send him unto *you*." Emphasis supplied. The Holy Spirit was sent to the disciples, and then the disciples were sent to work for those who needed to hear the good news of Jesus.

Let's look at John 16:7-11. Jesus is speaking, and He begins with interesting words: "Nevertheless I tell you the truth." Don't we understand that Jesus was in the habit of telling the truth? Apparently He was trying to give particular emphasis to what was to follow! "Nevertheless I tell you the truth; It is expedient for you that I go away: for if I go not away, the Comforter will not come unto you; but if I depart, I will send him unto you. And when he is come, he will reprove [or convict or convince] the world of sin, and of righteousness, and of judgment: Of sin, because they believe not on me; of righteousness, because I go to my Father, and ye see me no more; of judgment, because the prince of this world is judged."

So the Holy Spirit is sent to convict the world of its sinful condition. Our greatest need in accepting salvation is to realize our need. Our greatest need is to see our need! Otherwise we will not be motivated to come to Jesus and accept the salvation He offers. How many times have you tried to convince someone of his need and have experienced nothing but frustration? If the Holy Spirit is not present to bring conviction, the work of the preacher or teacher or parent or friend is futile. We cannot convince someone of his need. This is the work of the Holy Spirit on the person's heart. That is the work of the Holy Spirit, who knows the timetable for each individual.

In view of this fact, our work is twofold: (1) To invite the Spirit to bring conviction to those for whom we are concerned—but also (2) to invite the Spirit to cause us to cross paths with those whom He is already convicting.

This passage in John 16 assures us that the Holy Spirit will convict the world of sin. His work is not confined to any particular locality or group of people. It is a world mission, a world work. The Holy Spirit is no respecter of persons. "The Spirit of God is freely bestowed to enable every man to lay hold on the means of salvation. Thus Christ, 'the true Light,' 'lighteth every man that cometh into the world.'. . . Men fail of salvation through their own willful refusal of the gift of life."—*The Great Controversy*, p. 262.

"Those whom Christ commends in the judgment may have known little of theology, but they have cherished His principles. . . . Among the heathen are those who worship God ignorantly, those to whom the light is never brought by human instrumentality, yet they will not perish. Though ignorant of the written law of God, they have heard His voice speaking to them in nature, and have done the things that the law required. Their works are evidence that the Holy Spirit has touched their hearts, and they are recognized as the children of God.—*The Desire of Ages,* p. 638.

Jesus says here in John 16 that the Holy Spirit's work is to convince or convict of sin—and He gives His own definition for what constitutes sin. "Of sin, because they believe not on me." It doesn't say they are convicted of sin because they kill or lie or commit adultery. It doesn't say they are convicted of sin because they break God's law. It says they are convicted of sin because of lack of belief, or trust in Jesus Christ.

It is an easy thing to say that we believe in Christ, if we limit belief to simple mental assent. The Bible says that even the devils can agree on that. James 2:19 tells us that the devils believe—and tremble. In the days when Jesus was here on earth, sometimes His own disciples doubted His divinity. The priests and rulers appeared to have trouble recognizing Him as the Messiah. The common people, although they gladly heard His words, often questioned among themselves as to whether or not He was a prophet. But the devils believed and freely confessed that He was the Christ, the Holy One of God. See Mark 1:24, for example.

The sin of which the Holy Spirit brings conviction is the lack of *trust*—the lack of the faith that goes beyond mental assent and reaches down to the depths of the heart. The Holy Spirit brings the conviction that we have been living in rebellion against God, by maintaining control of our own lives—regardless of how moral our lives may have been. Through the Holy Spirit we are led to the faith relationship with Jesus that results in our trusting Him because we know Him. And because we know Him, we love Him and surrender to Him.

As human beings one of our greatest misunderstandings has to do with our true condition. "The heart is deceitful above all things, and desperately wicked: who can know it?" Jeremiah 17:9. It is it very easy to be deceived about our own condition. It may not be that hard for me to be aware of *your* sin! But my condition? That's another matter. And you may not have trouble discerning the sinful condition of those around you. But what about knowing the true picture of your own heart? It is only the Holy Spirit who can open our eyes to that.

THE HOLY SPIRIT AND CONVICTION 25

One day the parents of a problem child came to me for counseling. We were discussing the question of whether or not they had been too hard on their child, thereby causing some of his problems. We talked about the rule for discipline, that there is no limit to the discipline a child can take, so long as he knows he is loved and accepted. You can be extremely rigid in your demands, so long as a child knows he's loved and accepted. But you can be a complete marshmallow, and if the child doesn't know he's loved and accepted, he's going to have problems.

We talked about this rule, and the parents said, "Oh, our child knows he's loved and accepted. Sure he does." The mother nodded her head vigorously, and the father nodded too, and then he began nodding a little slower. And the first thing we knew, they were having an argument right there in my office as to whether or not their child knew he was loved and accepted.

Well, it happened to be obvious to those of us who knew the child from outside the home, that he did not feel loved and accepted. But the parents were the last to realize this. The heart is deceitful above all things. We are all experts at deceiving ourselves, and it is only the Holy Spirit who can convict us of sin and tear the masks from our faces, so we can realize our true condition and understand our deep need of the grace of God.

The Holy Spirit works to bring us to a sense of need and then to lift up Jesus as the answer to that need. One of the case histories of the convicting power of the Holy Spirit at work was on the day of Pentecost. It's recorded in Acts 2. Peter gave the sermon that day, and he began by giving a bit of history, a bit of genealogy, a bit of eschatology, and then a bit of prophecy from Joel. But when he got to the heart of his message, Jesus Christ, who had been crucified and then raised from the dead, it says that they were pricked in their hearts. And they interrupted Peter's sermon by giving their own altar call! They cried out, "Men and brethren, what shall we do?" Verse 37. What shall we do? They were obviously under conviction—and it happened when Jesus was uplifted!

This was the right kind of altar call! There were no soft

lights, no tear-jerking stories, no special music to work up the emotions. The Holy Spirit did His work, and 3,000 were converted that day.

We can be thankful for this first mighty work of the Holy Spirit in convicting of sin. But He doesn't stop there, and that is even greater good news! It is not enough for the sword of the Spirit to pierce to the heart and bring conviction, necessary as that work may be. In order to have salvation, we must not only see our need, but we must see the solution to that need. And the Holy Spirit keeps working with us. He does not wound and then leave us bruised and bleeding. He wounds that He may heal and bind up our wounds. He cuts deep with His sword that He may pour in oil and wine and bring complete restoration.

May the Holy Spirit today convict and convince you of the sin of not trusting in God, of living a life apart from Him, no matter how good or how bad that life may be. And how thankful we can be that when He has brought this conviction to our hearts that His work has only begun.

Chapter 4
The Holy Spirit and Conversion

When we are born in this world of sin, we are born with the absence of any joy in holiness or joy in communion with God. That's the problem of being born a sinner. Yet at the same time, we are born with an uncontrollable desire to worship. Even psychologists have discovered that human beings are born hopelessly religious. We are bound to worship something. We insist on worshiping something. People are invariably going to worship something or someone or themselves. That's why television and stardom are so popular. This need arises from the vacuum formed within the human heart which demands worship. But the vacuum is a God-shaped vacuum, and until we discover the truth of the gospel, we spend our time worshiping things or other people or ourselves, but are never satisfied.

No one is really born again until the Holy Spirit is able to lead him through conviction to the place where he is fed up with worshiping things or other people or himself. It is the work of the Holy Spirit to bring the sinner to the point of decision, to the realization that he needs something better and an understanding of what that something better is, so that the person can make an intelligent choice.

The second work of the Holy Spirit, the work of conversion or regeneration, follows for those who have experienced His first work—convincing them that they have a need. He convicts the world of sin, and then He works to bring the sinner to the point of conversion or new birth.

When it came to our first birth, we had no choice in the matter. Probably no one would argue that point. Some people are unhappy about the fact that they had no choice when it came to being born in a world of sin. But we're all in the same boat on that score. One thing is sure, God is not responsible for sin in the world; yet He is responsible for giving us existence, even though our parents had a hand in helping make it happen. So since God is the author of life, it is His responsibility that we were born in the first place.

Not only that, but it is God who is directly responsible for keeping our hearts beating right now. He is the one who keeps us alive during our time here on this earth, until we have used up whatever portion of three score years and ten that is our lot. And He is the one who has made sure that we *do* have a choice about one thing—our second birth. We had no choice in the matter of our first birth, but we do have a choice in the matter of our second birth, or being born again.

This is one area in which we find a difference between our lives and the life of Jesus when He was here on earth. Jesus had a choice about His first birth! We understand that Jesus, in counsel with His Father centuries before, made a deliberate decision to be born into a world of sin, to become our Saviour. Jesus was born differently from the way we are. Luke 1:35 tells us a little bit about it. It's an intriguing description, about as close as we're going to get to an explanation of the mystery of the incarnation of Jesus.

The angel comes bringing some big news to Mary, and Mary is confused. She understands the angel's message that she is to have a child, but she's wondering how it's going to happen. And the angel says, "The Holy Ghost shall come upon thee, and the power of the Highest shall overshadow thee: therefore also that holy thing which shall be born of thee shall be called the Son of God." Verse 35.

The same message was repeated to Joseph a few months later, when the angel came to quiet his fears concerning Mary's condition. "While he thought on these things, behold, the angel of the Lord appeared unto him in a dream, saying, Joseph, thou son of David, fear not to take unto thee Mary thy wife: for that which is conceived in her is of the Holy Ghost." Matthew 1:20.

Jesus was born with an inheritance different from ours, in that the Holy Spirit was His Father. He had a divine inheritance, a spiritual heredity, which we do not have. He was called "that holy thing"—and you and I were not born holy. But the fantastic truth is that the same experience Jesus had in His first birth, we can have in our second birth. We can come to the point where we decide whether or not we are going to be born of the Spirit. Ephesians 2:1, 4-7 talks about our being "quickened," made alive by the mighty power of God.

Now John 3 is the most complete chapter on the subject of the new birth. We'll look at only verses 3-5 at this time. Nicodemus, as you recall, had come for a secret interview with Jesus, and Jesus came right to the point of his need. "Jesus answered and said unto him, Verily, verily, I say unto thee, Except a man be born again, he cannot see the kingdom of God. Nicodemus saith unto him, How can a man be born when he is old? can he enter the second time into his mother's womb, and be born? Jesus answered, . . . Except a man be born of water and of the Spirit, he cannot enter into the kingdom of God."

It is interesting to note that even Jesus Himself respected the Holy Spirit's timetable for bringing about the new birth. Jesus didn't press or crowd Nicodemus. He didn't try to have him into the baptismal pool by the following Sabbath. He gave Nicodemus the most complete discourse on the subject of conversion and then left the Holy Spirit to do His work. For three years Nicodemus waited and pondered. Outwardly there was little change. But Jesus knew what He was doing, and the time came when Nicodemus gladly surrendered and accepted Jesus as his personal Saviour.

If you study the chapter on Nicodemus in the book, *The Desire of Ages* and put that together with the chapter on the woman at the well, you come up with a four-part definition for conversion. First of all, it is a supernatural work of the Holy Spirit. Second, it produces a change of attitude toward God. Third, it gives a new capacity for knowing God that we didn't even have before. And finally, it leads to a new life—leads to a willing obedience to all of God's requirements. Notice that it *leads* to a *willing* obedience. It is evidence that something has happened to change the inside—it is not a sudden resolution on the part of the sinner to clean up the outside. The emphasis is on discovering more and more that our will has come into harmony with God's will. And it is a process—it is not something that happens completely overnight.

There are two misunderstandings that often lead to discouragement among those who have recently committed themselves to God. One is the idea that conversion is an immediate, dramatic, total change of life. When a person has this idea and discovers the week after the week before, that there are some of the same temptations and tendencies and problems as before he was converted, it is often easy to assume he wasn't "really converted" after all, and to give up and wait for the next week of prayer or camp meeting or altar call. But notice carefully that what happens at conversion is primarily a change of attitudes, a change of direction.

The other misunderstanding is to have the idea that conversion is a one-time decision, and that once you've made that commitment, that's it for the rest of your life. But conversion is a daily matter—Jesus told us to take up our cross daily. "If you will seek the Lord and be converted every day . . . all your murmurings will be stilled, all your difficulties will be removed, all the perplexing problems that now confront you will be solved."—*Mount of Blessing,* p. 101.

Both of these mistaken ideas about conversion can be solved more easily if we remember what conversion really is. Romans 12:2 tells us, it is the renewing of our *minds*. Ephesians 4:22-24 speaks of being renewed in our minds. Regeneration and renewal have to do with the mind. It is not some magical process that drops into our lives from above. Rather it is a renewal of our thinking, our attitudes—a continuing education in the things of heaven. It is through our minds that we worship God. He never bypasses our minds in His dealing with us. It is the enemy of God and man who is willing to work by force, who really doesn't care what we think, so long as we submit to his control. But God wants only intelligent service.

This would be a major principle to watch out for in seeking to recognize the difference between the false and the true workings of the Holy Spirit. It is never the Holy Spirit that bypasses the mind and works only on the emotions or only on the outward actions of the individual.

There's a description of this process in *The Desire of Ages,* p.189. "In order to serve Him [God] aright, we must be born of the divine Spirit. This will purify the heart and renew the mind, giving us a new capacity for knowing and loving God."

How does the new birth happen? First Peter 1:23 gives a very significant clue. "Being born again, not of corruptible seed, but of incorruptible, by the word of God, which liveth and abideth for ever." So the new birth takes place through the operation of the Holy Spirit, working through God's Word. The Holy Spirit does not bypass God's Word. Second Peter 1:4 reminds us that it is through the Word of God that we become partakers of the divine nature. *Steps to Christ* gives a further description of the process. Jesus "died for us, and now He offers to take our sins and give us His righteousness. If you give yourself to Him, and accept Him as your Saviour, then, sinful as your life may have been, for His sake you are accounted righteous. Christ's character stands in place of your character, and you are accepted before God just as if you had not sinned."—Page 62. That's good news, isn't it? And that's what happens when we are born again.

Some have tried to keep the new birth as a completely legal transaction, a cleansing of the records in heaven, and nothing more. It is true that there is nothing *we* can do to save ourselves. But not every one who lives in this world will be saved, in spite of the fact that Jesus' sacrifice was enough for all. The sacrifice of Jesus is no good for the sinner until he accepts it, and our acceptance comes at the point of surrendering to the Holy Spirit as we see our need and our helplessness and our dependence upon God for salvation.

How does the new birth happen? Here's an amplification from *The Desire of Ages,* page 172. "Christ is constantly working upon the heart. Little by little, perhaps unconsciously to the receiver, impressions are made that tend to draw the soul to Christ. These may be received through meditating upon Him, through reading the Scriptures, or through hearing the word from the living preacher. Suddenly, as the Spirit comes with more direct appeal, the soul gladly surrenders itself to Jesus. By many this is called sudden conversion; but it is the result of long wooing by the Spirit of God."

We cannot convert someone else, but we can join in the work of the Holy Spirit by uplifting Jesus to those around us, by sharing the truths we have discovered in God's Word, and by encouraging those who are seeking for spiritual life to go where God's Word is to be presented.

Have you ever been converted? But have you been converted to God *today?* "None are living Christians unless they have a daily experience in the things of God.... Every living Christian will advance daily in the divine life. As he advances..., he experiences a conversion to God *every day."—Testimonies,* vol. 2, p. 505. Emphasis supplied.

Do you know if you have been converted? Do you know if you have been converted today? How can you know? The new life is not put on or worked up; it is sent down. But it is possible for us to know for ourselves whether or not we have received the gift from God, the work of the Holy Spirit in our lives. I'd like to include several points as to how we may know for ourselves whether or not we have experienced the new birth.

1. Is Jesus the center and focus of your life? "He that hath the Son hath life; and he that hath not the Son of God hath not life." 1 John 5:12. *Steps to Christ* gives two ways by which we can know that we are Christians: Of whom do we love to talk? Of whom do we love to think? See p. 58.

Sometimes it's easy to say we love Christ when someone asks if we love Him. But what's the real test? How much time do we actually spend in His presence, talking to Him and fellowshiping with Him? If Jesus is the center and focus of our lives, the whole life will revolve around our relationship with Him. He will be our most important priority. He will be the first One to whom we turn for companionship and the last One for whom we cannot find time.

2. Do you have a deep interest in God's Word? First Peter 2:2 tells us that as newborn babes we're going to desire the sincere

THE HOLY SPIRIT AND CONVERSION 33

(the Greek word means simple) milk of the Word. We're going to be hungry. While we may deliberately choose to spend time in God's Word, seeking to place ourselves in the atmosphere where the Holy Spirit works, until we are born again it may be uphill business to spend this time seeking spiritual nourishment. But one of the first things that happens to someone who is born is to get hungry! And the new capacity for knowing God is one of the gifts the Holy Spirit brings in His miracle of the new birth.

3. Do you have a meaningful prayer life? A born-again Christian will have a desire to communicate with God and with His Son Jesus Christ. He will seek to have a personal relationship with God. See John 17:3. Prayer is the breath of the soul, and it is essential that we breathe after we have been born. Spiritually or physically, life without breath is an extremely short-lived experience!

4. Do you have a daily experience in the things of God? "If any man will come after me, let him deny himself, and take up his cross daily, and follow me." Luke 9:23. The Christian life is not restricted to a couple of hours on Sabbath morning. It is a lifestyle, a daily and hourly walk with God.

5. Do you admit your sinful condition? Do you recognize the first work of the Holy Spirit to have been accomplished in your life? Have you been convicted of your sinfulness and your need of a Saviour? The closer we come to Jesus, the more we will realize our sinfulness, but at any time we feel that we are holy and have attained to righteousness, we are giving unmistakable evidence that we are in trouble!

This does not mean that we will continue to practice sin. But we are still sinners, still dependent upon Christ's cleansing power, for as long as life shall last. In our realization of weakness is our strength. "Are you in Christ? Not if you do not acknowledge yourself erring, helpless, condemned sinners."—*Testimonies,* vol. 5, p. 48.

6. Do you have inner peace? Peace is one of the first fruits of the Spirit to appear in the life of the newly born Christian. "Therefore being justified by faith, we have peace with God through our Lord Jesus Christ." Romans 5:1. Inner peace in

spite of whatever turmoil we face on the outside is one of the evidences that we have been born again.

7. And finally, do you have a desire to share with others the new life in Christ that you have found? *Steps to Christ* makes it very clear that "No sooner does one come to Christ than there is born in his heart a desire to make known to others what a precious friend he has found in Jesus; the saving and sanctifying truth cannot be shut up in his heart. If we are clothed with the righteousness of Christ . . . we shall not be able to hold our peace. . . . We shall have something to tell."—Page 78.

The new birth is a wonderful experience, and evidence of the miracle-working power of God. But we shouldn't stop there. One of the problems of the church called Laodicea is that its members too often accept the first and second works of the Holy Spirit. They are convicted that they are sinners, accept God's justifying grace, and experience the new birth. But there is more. "When souls are converted their salvation is not yet accomplished. They then have the race to run; the arduous struggle is before them . . . *'to fight the good fight of faith.'* . . . There is no release in this warfare; the battle is lifelong."—*My Life Today,* p. 313. Emphasis supplied.

Salvation includes more than justification. It also includes sanctification. It includes more than forgiveness—it also offers power for obedience, power for service. Which brings us to the next phase of the Holy Spirit's work, His work in cleansing the Christian. Keep reading!

Chapter 5
The Holy Spirit and Cleansing

Have you ever been afraid you had committed the unpardonable sin, even when you weren't sure exactly what the unpardonable sin is? Have you ever promised God that if He'd forgive you just one more time, you wouldn't do that particular thing again—and then you did it again and became afraid to even pray about it? Have you ever heard some particularly ominous sounding signs-of-the-times indication that Christ's coming is even nearer than you have thought—and it made you scared to death? If any of the above sounds familiar to you, there is wonderful good news in understanding the third work of the Holy Spirit, the cleansing of the Christian.

The cleansing work of the Holy Spirit is probably one of the most neglected, and therefore misunderstood, areas in the study of Christianity. There have been books written, songs composed, dramas presented that describe the process of conversion, taking a person step by step from a life of open rebellion to the initial surrender to the Lord Jesus. And there are an equal, if not greater, number of songs and books and plays dealing with the hope of heaven, the final rewards for God's children, and the soon return of Jesus.

But most of us are living somewhere in between these two events! Most church members have at some time made a commitment to Christ, or they probably would never have joined the church to begin with. And it doesn't take long to prove the point that we are not in heaven yet! To put it in the theologian's language, we've understood something about justification, and we're on our way toward glorification. But what about the area of sanctification? What about obedience and victory and overcoming and living the Christian life?

We have talked a lot about obedience in terms of *what*—what the law requires, what is right, and what is wrong, according to Scripture. But we have talked very little about *how*. And if you do not understand how obedience comes, then the greater your knowledge of what's right and what's wrong, the greater will be your discouragement.

Some have the impression that after the walk down to the altar, or the trip to the baptismal pool, everything will happen automatically—*if* they are sincere. For many young people, the assurance of salvation that came with justification was an extremely short-lived experience. Soon after, they discovered there were still many of the same problems, the same temptations, and the same weaknesses as before they had made the decision to invite Christ into their lives. In perplexity and embarrassment, they have often concluded that they were mistaken about being converted in the first place. And they wait in discouragement for another week of prayer or revival meeting or altar call, to try once again to find the magic formula that will make it work for them.

This predicament is by no means limited to young people. There are many older ones as well who have never discovered how to handle the sin problem they find in their lives.

In the early days of the advent church, our forefathers had an experience with the Lord Jesus that was deep and certain. They also hammered out doctrinal understandings that formed the basis for the Seventh-day Adventist Church. With the passing of time and a new generation taking the place of the founders of our church, often the new generation settled for the doctrinal truth only and did not seek the personal experience of faith that their parents had known. Thus formalism set in and the problem of salvation by works, leaving the church as dry as the hills of Gilboa.

By the time the third- and fourth-generation church members arrived on the scene, they not only did not know the personal relationship with Christ that their grandparents had

THE HOLY SPIRIT AND CLEANSING

known, but they failed to see the value of the doctrines of the church. Because of this factor, many young people leave the church, seeking for meaning to life in some other way.

Some who stay with the church, after trying and failing time and time again, finally conclude that sanctification is the work of a lifetime and hope that before they die they'll get in one good day. But with the evidence of the final smoke beginning to rise they get nervous and adjust their theology to match their experience, concluding that the defeated life is the best God has to offer.

In order to understand the work of the Holy Spirit in cleansing the heart from sin, it is essential to clearly define what *sin* is in the first place. And in order to overcome sin, it is vital not only to define sin, but to learn by what method sin is overcome.

Let's look first for a definition of *sin*. Have you ever heard of 1 John 3:4? "Sin is the transgression of the law." That is probably one that we quote most often. But let's put with that two other texts: Romans 14:23, "Whatsoever is not of faith is sin," and John 16:9, where Jesus talks about the work of the Holy Spirit in convicting the world of sin. He says, "Of sin, because they believe not on me."

If sin were nothing more than breaking the law, then all we would have to do to be saved would be what?—keep the law. Is keeping the law what saves us? Is the sin problem solved by morality, or does the sinner need a Saviour?

Consider for a moment how sin began in the first place. Have you ever been in on a discussion of whether Eve sinned when she touched the fruit or when she tasted the fruit or perhaps back when she wandered from Adam's side? Don't forget that sin began with Lucifer—not with Eve! And what was Lucifer's problem? Did he begin by working on Sabbath or stealing mangoes? What does the Bible say about it? Read it in Isaiah 14:13, 14. "Thou hast said in thine heart, I will ascend into heaven, I will exalt my throne above the stars of God: . . . I will be like the most High." Lucifer sinned when he stopped depending upon God and started depending upon himself. It happened when he broke away from the trusting relationship he had with his Creator and tried to be his own god.

And so it was with Eve. Satan presented to her the same temptation that had led to his own downfall—"Ye shall be as gods."

So the basis of sin is self-dependence which results in separation from God. Breaking the commandments is the *result* of sin. Go back to 1 John 3:4 again, and look at the whole verse. "Whosoever committeth sin transgresseth *also* the law." Emphasis supplied. Whoever separates from the dependent relationship with God and depends on himself is also going to break the commandments, "for sin [living apart from God] is the transgression of the law." Since the bottom line of the law of God is God-dependence, not self-dependence, then, whenever you separate from God and try to be your own god, transgression of the rest of the law will inevitably result.

Now the basic premise of righteousness by faith in Jesus is that mankind has no righteousness apart from Jesus. "Sinful man can find hope and righteousness only in God, and no human being is righteous any longer than he has faith in God and maintains a vital connection with Him."—*Testimonies to Ministers,* p. 367.

In John 15:5 Jesus says, "Without me ye can do nothing." And Philippians 4:13 says, "I can do all things through Christ." Put those two verses together, and you have in a nutshell the message of salvation by faith. If without Christ we can do nothing, but with Him we can do all things, then all that is left for us to do is to get with Him. And John 17:3 still says, "This is life eternal, that they might know thee the only true God, and Jesus Christ, whom thou hast sent."

The way we get to be sinners in the first place is to be born. Psalm 58:3: "The wicked are estranged from the womb: they go astray as soon as they be born." And Psalm 51:5: "Behold, I was shapen in iniquity; and in sin did my mother conceive me." Jesus told Nicodemus in John 3 that unless we are born again, we cannot even see the kingdom of heaven. Therefore, something must have been wrong with our first birth.

Sin is separation from God and self-dependence. Righteousness is available only through connection with Jesus and the faith relationship with Him. No one is righteous any longer

THE HOLY SPIRIT AND CLEANSING 39

than they maintain that relationship with Christ. And the relationship with Christ is maintained by a daily coming to Him for communion, by daily surrendering ourselves to His control instead of trying to control ourselves. This means spending prime time in fellowship with Him.

The beginning of this life of seeking Jesus day by day happens at the point of conversion. At conversion, we are given a new heart, which is manifest in a new capacity to know and love God. We also receive a new attitude toward God, as we noticed in the previous chapter. But does that mean that from the point of conversion onward, we will never sin again, never fall again, never fail again? And right here comes the potential for major misunderstandings.

A "new theology" that has made the rounds in recent years says: "Of course we will sin and fall and fail after conversion. In fact, we will continue sinning and falling and failing right up to the point of glorification. If we don't sin knowingly, we're sure to sin unknowingly." And so the answer to the dilemma offered by the proponents of this theory is this: "Don't worry about sin, since it is our nature—until we are glorified. The answer to the problem is to trust in the sacrifice of Christ in our behalf and believe that His righteousness will cover us until He comes again and removes the sin problem from our hearts."

Then there are Adventists who say that you lose your salvation every time you sin or fall or fail. They maintain that if you are "really converted" and "really sincere" that you will experience nothing but victory from the moment of conversion onward. Those who accept this view believe that there is a great deal of human effort necessary toward fighting sins in order to keep from falling and failing, that there is the necessity for constant watchfulness against temptation and gritting your teeth and trying hard not to do wrong things. They do not deny that if you sin, you can still come back to God and seek for forgiveness, although some of the more rigid among them argue from the sanctuary services in the Old Testament times that there is no forgiveness available for "known" sins—only for sins that you accidentally stumble into.

The arguments between these two extremes are long and

complicated, with much time spent discussing things that have to do with the nature of Christ and perfection and so on. But I would like to make an attempt to describe a third option. And I would also like to keep it as simple as possible, leaving the deep theological waters for some other time.

Let's try a question-and-answer format for a few pages, as we examine some of these issues.

1. Do people who have made a sincere, complete surrender to the Lord Jesus Christ ever sin again?

Let's go to the Bible for the answer. What about the disciples of Jesus? They walked and talked with Him for three and a half years and even in the upper room the night before the crucifixion were still bickering and arguing about who was going to be the greatest. Had they been converted? Well, Jesus told them their names were written in the book of life. See Luke 10:20. They had been healing the sick, cleansing the lepers, casting out devils, and raising the dead in the name and power of Jesus. But they still had a sin problem.

Look at the Old Testament saints. Moses had been converted. He had talked to God on the mountain and was so assured of his eternal salvation that he offered it to God as incentive in his intercession for the wayward Israelites. But he sinned on the very borders of the Promised Land.

David was called a man after God's own heart at one time, but he committed murder and adultery in connection with his relationship to Bethsheba. Gideon, under the control of the Spirit of God, took 300 men with torches and pitchers and won a mighty victory for the people of Israel. Then he became so impressed with what he had just done that he grew dissatisfied with his job as a farmer and decided to be a priest, a prerogative reserved for the Levites.

Abraham was called the friend of God. He trusted God enough to leave his home and country and go out to an unknown place. He dared to dialog with God about the fate of Sodom. But he lied to more than one man about his wife, Sarah, being merely his sister.

Elijah was fearless for God on Mount Carmel, but his faith failed that very night in the face of a woman's threats. Noah

THE HOLY SPIRIT AND CLEANSING

stood firm for 120 years while he built the ark amid the scorn and jeers of an unbelieving world, but soon after the flood you find him in a drunken stupor.

Then there are some who were prophets of God, and yet so weak and waffling that we wonder how they could have been given the title—such as Samson and Jonah and Balaam.

So do people who have made a sincere surrender to the Lord Jesus ever sin again? Yes, they do.

2. Does that mean that obedience is impossible?

Here is where misunderstanding often comes in considering this topic. If all these Bible characters sinned and failed, even after they were converted, does that mean there's no hope? Is obedience impossible? Or unnecessary? Or unimportant? No, *NO*, and **NO!**

Underline it in your mind. Obedience is possible. Obedience is necessary. And obedience is extremely important!

3. Were there any Bible characters who apparently did not fall and fail and sin after coming to Christ?

Yes, the good news is that there were. There were a few. Enoch. Daniel. Elisha. Only a few. Enough to prove that it is possible to lock in on the initial surrender to God and never waver from that position throughout an entire lifetime in a world of sin.

4. Then what makes the difference? If failure is not inevitable, why does it happen?

The answer lies in what we might call the "so long as" principle. When we come to Christ in the first place and surrender to Him, we are as surrendered as we will ever be! Surrender is never partial. It's all or nothing. Either you are surrendered, or you are not surrendered. Either you are depending on God or you are depending on yourself. There is no middle ground.

So long as we are surrendered to God, sin has no power over us. Not only sinful deeds, but sinful desires are gone. *The Desire of Ages,* page 668 is the classic on that. "All true obedience comes from the heart. It was heart work with Christ. And if we consent, He will so identify Himself with our thoughts and aims, so blend our hearts and minds into conformity to His will, that when obeying Him we shall be but carrying out our own impulses. The will, refined and sanctified, will find its highest delight in doing His service. When we know God as it is our privilege to know Him, our life will be a life of continual obedience. Through an appreciation of the character of Christ, through communion with God, sin will become hateful to us."

All that is available to us is available right from the beginning of the Christian life. God isn't in the business of doling out His power by degrees and only allowing so much victory according to how long we have been in His service.

If we were to trace the work of the Holy Spirit in cleansing the Christian, beginning at the time of conversion, it would work something like this: When a person is converted, he has experienced surrender for the first time. Surrender is giving up on himself and transferring his self-dependence to God-dependence. If he were to stay in this stance the rest of his days and depend wholly upon God all of the time, and never upon himself, he would never fall or fail or sin again.

But many of us have discovered that in the growing Christian life, we have not known how to stay in the surrendered stance, and so we fall and fail and sin and need to come again and again with confession and repentance. This means we have not stayed locked into the surrendered stance. We have drifted back and forth between depending totally upon God and depending upon ourselves.

The cleansing work of the Holy Spirit takes the Christian from the moment of conversion and patiently leads him in the experience of surrender, taking him just as fast as possible to a time when he will stay surrendered to God all the time, instead of just part of the time. The growth in the Christian life is in the *constancy* of surrender.

The Holy Spirit's goal for us is to bring us to the point of constant surrender, or what we might call absolute surrender, to the place where we will never again depend upon self, no matter what the circumstances. And for most of us, this involves time.

Steps to Christ, page 18 describes this process. "The Saviour said, 'Except a man be born from above,' unless he shall receive a new heart, new desires, purposes, and motives, *leading to* a

THE HOLY SPIRIT AND CLEANSING 43

new life, 'he cannot see the kingdom of God.' " Emphasis supplied.

The inward change *leads to* a changed life in terms of behavior. But there is often a process involved. There are times when we take our eyes off Christ and once again depend on ourselves without realizing it, and then we are surprised into sin. But the basis of our continued assurance of salvation is in the daily coming to Christ, spending time in His Word and in prayer, and inviting His control of our lives. Within that framework, the Holy Spirit works to lead us just as fast as possible to the place where we will depend upon Him every moment of every day.

It is of utmost importance to understand the difference between the momentary lapse in keeping the eyes fixed upon Christ, and the deliberate choice to again walk separate from God, independent of His control. The first can happen without our conscious choice. The second comes only as we choose to separate from God and no longer seek Him day by day.

For the Christian who begins each day in fellowship and communion and commitment to Christ, it is still possible at any given moment to take the eyes off Christ and to begin depending upon self. When that happens transgression is inevitable. It may be only inward desire for sin for the strong person, or it may also include outward wrong actions for the weak. But too often we find ourselves depending on ourselves, and instead of fleeing to Christ for His pardon and power, we think we can handle things on our own, and that is the basis of defeat.

Notice three quotations from the inspired commentary which should bring hope to those who are still in the stages, still experiencing the Holy Spirit's cleansing work, without having yet reached the point of absolute surrender.

First, from the *Review and Herald* of May 12, 1896: "If one who daily communes with God errs from the path, if he turns a moment from looking steadfastly unto Jesus, it is not because he sins willfully; for when he sees his mistake, he turns again, and fastens his eyes upon Jesus, and the fact that he has erred, does not make him less dear to the heart of God."

Steps to Christ, page 64: "There are those who have known the pardoning love of Christ and who really desire to be children of God, yet they realize that their character is imperfect, their life faulty, and they are ready to doubt whether their hearts have been renewed by the Holy Spirit. To such I would say, Do not draw back in despair. We shall often have to bow down and weep at the feet of Jesus because of our shortcomings and mistakes, but we are not to be discouraged. Even if we are overcome by the enemy, we are not cast off, not forsaken and rejected of God. No; Christ is at the right hand of God, who also maketh intercession for us. . . . If you will but yield yourself to Him, He that hath begun a good work in you will carry it forward to the day of Jesus Christ. Pray more fervently; believe more fully. As we come to distrust our own power, let us trust the power of our Redeemer, and we shall praise Him who is the health of our countenance."

And this one from *Prophets and Kings,* page 589, in the chapter describing Joshua, clothed in filthy garments, being accused before God: "But while the followers of Christ have sinned, they have not given themselves up to be controlled by the satanic agencies."

The cleansing work of the Holy Spirit is to bring us to the moment-by-moment surrender to God, within the framework of our continued seeking of God day by day. The work of the Holy Spirit in cleansing the heart is not for the purpose of saving us. It is to save us from our self-dependence, that God may be glorified in us. The cleansing work of the Holy Spirit is not what saves us—but because we are in a saving relationship, the Holy Spirit can work to cleanse our hearts.

We do not believe in a limited salvation. It is God's plan for His people to be delivered from sin completely and totally. We may still have to live in a world of sin, and we may still experience the effects of sin, in death and suffering and pain. But we are not bound to continue to live *in* sin. Sin does not have to live in us. The *Review and Herald* of September 19, 1899, declares, "All sin, from the least to the greatest, may be overcome by the Holy Spirit's power." And the *Review and Herald* of November 12, 1914, says, "The religion of Christ means more than the forgiveness of sins. It means that sin is taken away, and that the life is filled with the Spirit."

The Desire of Ages, page 671 says: "Sin could be resisted and overcome only through the mighty agency of the Third Person of the Godhead, who would come with no modified energy, but in the fullness of divine power. It is the Spirit that makes effectual what has been wrought out by the world's Redeemer. It is by the Spirit that the heart is made pure. Through the Spirit the believer becomes a partaker of the divine nature. Christ has given His Spirit as a divine power to overcome all hereditary and cultivated tendencies to evil."

First John 1:9 says, "If we confess ours sins, he is faithful and just to forgive us our sins, and to *cleanse us* from all unrighteousness." Emphasis supplied.

This cleansing work of the Holy Spirit has been called His greatest work. You'll find this declaration in *Testimonies,* vol. 7, p. 143. "The greatest manifestation of its [Holy Spirit] power is seen in human nature brought to the perfection of the character of Christ."

This brings us to one final issue: How does it happen? What part of the work does God expect us to do? What part does He do *for* us through the Holy Spirit's cleansing work?

We've touched on the *how* already, but let's underscore it to be sure the issues are clear. Our part is to seek the Lord and be converted every day. Our part is to spend that thoughtful hour in contemplation of the life of Christ, especially the closing scenes, that by beholding Him we may become changed. Throughout the day, we may become aware of having turned away from depending on Him. We may realize we have taken our eyes off Christ. Often the realization comes when we find ourselves suddenly defeated. What do we do? We "turn again." We go to God immediately for pardon and for power. And we continue to seek Him day by day, regardless of the lapses in our behavior and performance. For it is only through the Holy Spirit's power that we can ever hope to overcome.

How long will it take before we are completely cleansed from sin? How long before we no longer turn from depending upon Christ, even for a moment? It's not a matter of the calendar. For

Elisha it seemed to happen overnight. For Jacob, it took twenty years. But His promise is sure, if we continue to walk with Him, "He who began a good work in you will carry it on to completion." Philippians 1:6, NIV. As we continue in relationship and fellowship and communion with Christ day by day, as we daily seek Him to lead us to surrender our will and our lives to Him, He will bring us as fast as possible to the crisis of absolute surrender, and that's the subject for the next chapter.

Chapter 6
The Crisis of Surrender

Jacob would have made a good Pentagon man. He was a master of strategy. He knew how to manipulate circumstances to his own ends. He was sly. He had sharpened wits with his Uncle Laban for twenty years and had finally outmaneuvered even him. Now he was on his way home to see his father, but on the way he had to pass through his brother Esau's country.

Jacob had good reason to believe that Esau might still be upset from the last contact they had had when Jacob had gotten away with the birthright. So he was feeling nervous. He divided his family and servants into two units, so that if one was captured, the other might escape. He even made sure to get his favorite wife, Rachel, into the group that had the best chance of getting away. He had sent peace offerings to his brother, hoping to soften the memory of their last encounter. And now he turned aside to pray! He certainly was taking every precaution!

Jacob was facing the crisis of his life—the crisis of surrender. The crisis of surrender could have other labels for it, such as the crisis of cleansing or the crisis of filling by the Holy Spirit. It is a subject that is sometimes debated, because some insist that conversion and the crisis of surrender must happen at the same time. But we take the position on the basis of Bible case histories such as Jacob, that there may be a lapse in time between conversion and the crisis of surrender. In fact, this is the case more often than not.

This is not to say that conversion does not involve surrender. But the human heart has a way of not staying in the surren-

48 YOUR FRIEND, THE HOLY SPIRIT

dered stance and of swinging back and forth between total dependence upon God and dependence upon ourselves. This is a painful reality and leads to a painful crisis—the crisis of absolute surrender.

Now we know that all conversions are not alike. One person has a tremendous upheaval, while for another person conversion is almost imperceptible. Sometimes, perhaps, we overstate this difference, as second-, third-, or fourth-generation church members. We like to clutch to our hearts the idea that conversion can be imperceptible, and you may never know the time or the date or the occasion. But notice this description of conversion from the book *The Desire of Ages,* page 172: "Christ is constantly working upon the heart. Little by little, perhaps unconsciously to the receiver, impressions are made that tend to draw the soul to Christ. These may be received through meditating upon Him, through reading the Scriptures, or through hearing the word from the living preacher. Suddenly, as the Spirit comes with more direct appeal, the soul gladly surrenders itself to Jesus." Did you catch the transition from "little by little" to "suddenly"? The passage continues: "By many this is called sudden conversion; but it is the result of long wooing by the Spirit of God."

So there is even a process involved leading up to the point of conversion. It may be slow, imperceptible, gradual, and little by little. But suddenly there comes a point of crisis.

Perhaps no one would question that it is the will of God that the initial experience of surrender be a lasting surrender. It isn't God's purpose for there to be a gap between the two. But as we noticed in the last chapter, in the lives of many godly people, there has been a growing process, a matter of time and trial and error before they came to the place of staying locked into the surrendered stance.

But there's one thing that we can all agree on, and that is that if conversion got by you imperceptibly, and you're one of these people who could never point to a time or date or even year, you've just simply been a good church member all your life—we can all agree that absolute surrender is not going to get by you that same way. Why? Because of *Steps to Christ,*

THE CRISIS OF SURRENDER 49

page 43. "The warfare against self is the greatest battle that was ever fought. The yielding of self, surrendering all to the will of God, requires a struggle; but the soul must submit to God before it can be renewed in holiness." If you are still discovering times in your life when you depend on yourself and end up in defeat, then there is a big crisis that will be coming your way—the crisis of surrender.

What kind of crisis is it? It is a big crisis for those of us who have failed the little crises. This is true of life at large. If I fail to learn my multiplication tables, I'm headed for a big crisis when I try to pass college math. If I've never learned to dog paddle, I'm in for a big crisis when I try to swim the English Channel. If I'm nervous about jumping off the back porch, I will be in for a big crisis if I ever take up sky diving.

Someone may think it's only a little thing to smoke one cigarette. But one day some people face a big crisis—lung cancer. Someone else may discover a way to get around dropping a dime in the pay telephone in order to make a phone call. A little crisis. But one day comes the charge of grand theft. No one goes from the innocence of the newborn to becoming a hardened criminal in one big jump. It takes time. It involves a process.

The reason Peter found himself clutching the ground and grinding his face in the dirt in Gethsemane and wishing he could die was not the result of a single moment. He had failed in the smaller crisis on the lake, when he thought he could walk on water by himself. He had failed in the crisis over the temple tax coins. He had failed to see the place of the cross in Christ's mission and had been rebuked by Jesus in strong words, "Get thee behind me, Satan." He had thought he could fight his own battles and managed to slice off Malchus's ear before Jesus stopped him. *The Desire of Ages,* page 382 says that if Peter had learned what Jesus tried to teach him in the smaller crises, he would not have failed when the big test came. "Day by day God instructs His children. By the circumstances of the daily life He is preparing them to act their part upon that wider stage to which His providence has appointed them. It is the issue of the daily test that determines their victory or defeat in life's great crisis."

So there comes a series of smaller events, all based upon one issue: Am I going to try to handle it myself, or am I going to trust God to handle it for me? The smaller events come along, and if I continue to fall and fail, I can plan on a big wrestling with the angel some night by the brook Jabbok.

Evidently some of those who appear to have done it right all along, such as Enoch and Daniel and Elisha, must have passed their tests on a smaller scale.

It is possible to flunk the small tests and hardly be aware of it. Esau found that to be true. He came home one day and was hungry. So he sold his birthright for a kettle of lentils. Who would ever think that a momentary impulse over a pot of lentils would be that big a deal? But notice this comment about Esau. "Esau passed the crisis of his life without knowing it. What he regarded as a matter worthy of scarcely a thought was the act which revealed the prevailing traits of his character. It showed his choice, showed his true estimate of that which was sacred and which should have been sacredly cherished."—Ellen G. White Comments, *S.D.A. Bible Commentary,* vol. 1, pp. 1094, 1095.

And so we come to Jacob. Jacob was converted at Bethel, as he was fleeing from his father's home. He hadn't done well on the smaller tests up to that point, either. He had resorted to deception, trying to help God out in obtaining the promised birthright. But something happened at Bethel. And Jacob surrendered to God.

Then for twenty years he continued with the problem of self-effort. He had a relationship with God, yes. But he also kept interferring with the Lord's control and trying to make things happen in his own way. By the evening of the struggle at Jabbok, he had exhausted his own resources. He had tried everything—now everything was at stake. And suddenly he knew that his efforts were not enough. He began to seek the Lord in a way that he hadn't before. And the Lord came near to respond to Jacob's plea for help.

Jacob feels a hand on his shoulder. He is sure it is an enemy. He begins to struggle. He spends the entire night doing exactly what he has done for the last twenty years. Every time for twenty years that God has placed His hand on Jacob, Jacob has misunderstood and begun fighting for himself. He does it again—and continues the struggle until the dawning of the day.

And when the day finally dawned, Jacob, instead of fighting God, clung to Him. I like that, don't you? From the night of wrestling, Jacob came forth a different man. "Self-confidence had been uprooted."—*Patriarchs and Prophets,* p. 208. And the crisis of Jacob's life, the crisis of surrender, had finally happened.

It takes time. It takes time to transform the human to the divine. Just as it takes time to degrade those formed in the image of God to the brutal or the satanic. It takes time either direction. Time had done its work in the life of Jacob, and he was never the same again.

Our greatest strength is realized when we feel and acknowledge our weakness. Christ connects fallen men and women, in their weakness and helplessness, with the source of Infinite power. What changed about Jacob that night? He realized that for twenty years he had been doing that which God did not expect him to do. For twenty years he had been trying, in his own strength, to live up to the promises he had made to God at Bethel. Now he finally understood that surrender was the way to victory.

When God comes to us and places His hand on our shoulder, wouldn't it be wonderful to recognize Him immediately as a friend, rather than an enemy? "It was by self-surrender and confiding faith that Jacob gained what he had failed to gain by conflict in his own strength. God thus taught His servant that divine power and grace alone could give him the blessing he craved. Thus it will be with those who live in the last days. As dangers surround them, and despair seizes upon the soul, they must depend solely upon the merits of the atonement. We can do nothing of ourselves. In all our helpless unworthiness we must trust in the merits of the crucified and risen Saviour. None will ever perish while they do this."—*Ibid.,* p. 203.

Whatever form that great crisis may take in your life, you can be assured that if you continue to seek the relationship of trust and communion with Jesus day by day, you will be brought to that crisis. And once that crisis is past in your life, you will never be the same again.

"Such will be the experience of God's people in their final struggle with the powers of evil. God will test their faith, their perseverance, their confidence in His power to deliver them. Satan will endeavor to terrify them with the thought that their cases are hopeless; that their sins have been too great to receive pardon. They will have a deep sense of their shortcomings, and as they review their lives their hopes will sink. But remembering the greatness of God's mercy, and their own sincere repentance, they will plead His promises made through Christ to helpless, repenting sinners. Their faith will not fail because their prayers are not immediately answered. They will lay hold of the strength of God, as Jacob laid hold of the Angel, and the language of their souls will be, 'I will not let Thee go, except Thou bless me.' "—*Ibid.*, p. 202.

The struggle will be intense. The enemy will do all in his power to cause you to give in to fear and discouragement. But just remember, when the hand of God is placed on your shoulder, it's not an enemy. It's the best Friend you've ever had.

Chapter 7
The Holy Spirit and the Commission for Service

One time I was at a camp meeting where we had been discussing the final phase of the work of the Holy Spirit, what could be called the baptism of the Holy Spirit. And we had called it the baptism of the Holy Spirit! Some in the audience were uncomfortable with that phrase and came around after the meeting and asked, "Why do you keep saying baptism of the Holy Spirit?" Well, in talking a little further, it became apparent that in their background, the phrase "baptism of the Holy Spirit" had always been associated with the type of meeting where people scream and shout and foam at the mouth and roll in the aisles! But the phrase is straight out of Scripture, nonetheless!

The four gospels quote John the Baptist in speaking of the baptism of the Holy Spirit. See Matthew 3:11; Mark 1:8; Luke 3:16; and John 1:33. The four references read almost the same, so let's look at only one of them. Luke 3:16; "John answered, saying unto them all, I indeed baptize you with water; but one mightier than I cometh, the latchet of whose shoes I am not worthy to unloose: he shall baptize you with the Holy Ghost and with fire."

The baptism of the Holy Spirit is also spoken of in Acts 1:4, 5, 8. We'll come back to that passage in a few minutes. But Acts 11:16 also refers to the baptism of the Holy Spirit, where Peter recalls the promise Jesus gave concerning it.

There are other references to the experience that use other words to describe it, such as being filled with the Spirit, being endued with the Spirit, receiving the gift of the Holy Spirit, and receiving the promise of the Father, yet all of these passages refer to the same thing—the ultimate work of the Holy Spirit in the life of the Christian.

In this chapter we'd like to establish three truths concerning the fourth work of the Holy Spirit, and then in the following chapter we will go into the study of how we receive it.

1. You Will Know When You Have Received the Baptism of the Holy Spirit.

Let's go back to Acts 1:4, 5, 8. Jesus has led His disciples up the mountain pathway for their last, in-person contact with Him before He returns to His Father. "And, being assembled together with them, commanded them that they should not depart from Jerusalem, but wait for the promise of the Father, which, saith he, ye have heard of me. For John truly baptized with water; but ye shall be baptized with the Holy Ghost not many days hence." "But ye shall receive power, after that the Holy Ghost is come upon you: and ye shall be witnesses unto me both in Jerusalem, and in all Judaea, and in Samaria, and unto the uttermost part of the earth."

The experience of being filled with the Holy Ghost, of being baptized with power from on high, is a definite experience, of which one may know of a certainty whether or not he has received it.

After the conversion of the Christian, there begins the process of cleansing—the third work of the Spirit which we have already studied. This work involves not only the overcoming of sin and self-dependence, but also the time to develop the positive Christian virtues. The fruits of the Spirit come during the third work of the Holy Spirit. And it takes time to grow fruit. "The precious graces of the Holy Spirit are not developed in a moment."—*Review and Herald,* April 28, 1910.

Then comes the crisis of surrender, the time when the Christian is finally finished with self-effort and self-dependence. And it is only then that the Holy Spirit can be given in His fullness.

But you will know when you have received it. Jesus told His

disciples to wait in Jerusalem until they were baptized with the Holy Ghost. Obviously, He expected something definite and expected them to know when it happened. Another reference on the same point is in Luke 24:49, where Jesus said, "Behold, I send the promise of my Father upon you: but tarry ye in the city of Jerusalem, until ye be endued with power from on high." If the disciples had not been able to know when the baptism of the Holy Ghost had come, they might still be waiting there in Jerusalem.

We also find support for this premise in Acts 19:2, where the apostle Paul came to a group of believers in Ephesus, and "he said unto them, Have ye received the Holy Ghost since ye believed?" Their answer was definite, and almost humorous, for "they said unto him, We have not so much as heard whether there be any Holy Ghost." And Paul went on to instruct them. They were rebaptized in the name of Jesus, and then the Holy Ghost was poured out upon them.

Suppose the apostle Paul could come to you today and ask, "Have you received the Holy Spirit?" What would you say? The Bible principle is that at least you should be able to know, one way or the other!

2. The Baptism of the Holy Spirit Is a Work of the Spirit That Is Separate and Distinct From Conversion.

When a person is born again, his name is entered in the book of life, and he is assured of salvation through faith in Jesus, so long as he continues to accept it. But he still might not yet be fitted for God's service to the extent that God has in mind for him. He still has growing to do. He has experienced the early work of the Spirit, for Romans 8:9 says, "Now if any man have not the Spirit of Christ, he is none of his." But he does not yet have the fullness of the Spirit in His ultimate work.

We have already noticed the words of Jesus to His disciples, telling them to tarry in Jerusalem until they received the Holy Ghost. Were the disciples converted? Sometimes people argue about that and say that when Jesus said to Peter, "When you are converted, strengthen the brethren," that was evidence that Peter did not become converted until after he denied Christ on the night prior to the crucifixion. As we have noticed earlier, that's hard to prove from Scripture, for Peter's name was in the book of life by the time of sending out of the seventy. There is no question that Peter fell, and his repentance was of such a deep nature that he was brought to his crisis of surrender. But however you wish to chart Peter's experience, you will have to admit that by the time he met with Jesus in Galilee, Peter was a changed man. And yet there was still a waiting time involved before the filling with the Spirit.

Look at Acts 19:2 once more. Paul said, "Have ye received the Holy Ghost *since ye believed?*" Emphasis supplied. So he was talking to believers. He wasn't talking to the unconverted, to heathen, to atheists. These people had been baptized with "John's baptism." Was there something wrong with John's baptism? Didn't John believe in Jesus? Didn't John believe in the Holy Spirit? Why, we're told that John the Baptist was filled with the Spirit from his mother's womb. But there was still a further work the Spirit wanted to do in their lives.

Let's examine one more instance from the book of Acts, concerning a group of believers in Samaria. You recall that Philip was one of the deacons in the early church, chosen because he was a man full of the Holy Spirit. He did not content himself with passing the offering plate and locking up the church after the Sabbath services. He began preaching.

So he preached to the Samaritans "the things concerning the kingdom of God, and the name of Jesus Christ, [and] they were baptized, both men and women." Acts 8:12.

Here then is a group of people baptized in the name of the Lord Jesus Christ; obviously they are people who have been born again. Or at least *some* of them must have been born again! Maybe there were a few who just went along with their peers. But the record continues in verses 14-17: "When the apostles which were at Jerusalem heard that Samaria had received the word of God, they sent unto them Peter and John: who, when they were come down, prayed for them, that they might receive the Holy Ghost: (For as yet he was fallen upon *none* of them: only they were baptized in the name of the Lord

THE HOLY SPIRIT AND THE COMMISSION FOR SERVICE

Jesus.) Then laid they their hands on them, and they received the Holy Ghost." So here again you have the definite experience of receiving the baptism of the Holy Ghost, which is separate from, and distinct from the initial experience of conversion.

The one exception to this rule may have been Cornelius, who received the Holy Spirit even before he was baptized. However, even for Cornelius, the evidence is that he had been converted and surrendered to God according to the light he had already received, even before Peter came with the message of greater light.

There are many references in the inspired commentary to the same truth. We will notice just one or two. "We must be endued with power from on high; we must have the baptism of the Holy Spirit before we leave this place."—*Review and Herald,* June 24, 1884. This was an excerpt from an address given to ministers and gospel workers, many of whom were obviously already converted. And again, in a similar sermon, "We must have the holy unction from God; we must have the baptism of the Holy Spirit."—*Ibid.,* December 15, 1885.

3. The Purpose of the Baptism of the Holy Spirit Is Not to Make Us Holy, or to Make Us Happy, But to Make Us Useful

If you examine all of the material on the subject of the Holy Spirit's fourth work, you will discover that in every case, the purpose is for witness, outreach, service. His fourth work is to commission us for service. The baptism of the Spirit is given to further the work of God on earth. It is not given for the purpose of cleansing—that will have been accomplished under the previous work of the Holy Spirit. And it is for a purpose far deeper than just making us feel joyous and cheerful.

Notice again in Acts 1:8 the words of Jesus: "Ye shall receive power, after that the Holy Ghost is come upon you: and *ye shall be witnesses unto me.*" Emphasis supplied. This is not to say that we won't be involved in sharing what Christ has done in our lives, even from the time of conversion. The demoniacs of

Gadara went back to tell what Jesus had done for them immdeiately after they had been delivered from the controlling demons.

But the power for witnessing on the larger scale, in taking the gospel to the world, can come only under the empowering of the Spirit. Could we suggest that the primary evidence that anyone has been baptized with the Holy Spirit is not the gift of tongues or prophesying or wind or fire. It is a passion for saving the lost. It is a burden for reaching others with the good news of the gospel of Jesus Christ. And if I am content to be an average church member, to simply polish the dust off of my pew week by week and never go out of my way to reach out or witness, then that is probably one of the greatest evidences that I have not yet received the fullness of the Spirit's work.

Sometimes we have gotten the idea as Seventh-day Adventists that the baptism of the Holy Spirit is reserved for the time of the latter rain. And it is certainly true that the Spirit will be poured out upon God's people at that time. But we are not expected to fold our hands and wait for the final outpouring of God's Spirit on the earth. It is our privilege to pray for it and seek for it and study how to receive it even *now*.

We "are to wrestle with God in earnest prayer for a baptism of the Holy Spirit, that [we] may meet the needs of a world perishing in sin."—*Review and Herald,* March 31, 1910.

"We need people who realize their soul poverty and who will earnestly seek for the endowment of the Holy Spirit. As we talk of the matchless charms of the divine Redeemer, our hearts will be melted and endued by the Holy Spirit. We must be clothed with power from on high by the baptism of the Holy Spirit. There is help for us no other way."—*Ibid.,* April 5, 1892.

"If we are to learn of Christ, we must pray as the apostles prayed when the Holy Spirit was poured upon them. We need a baptism of the Spirit of God."—*Ibid.,* November 11, 1909.

And one more statement, found in *Evangelism,* page 701. "The descent of the Holy Spirit upon the church is looked forward to as in the future; but it is the privilege of the church to have it now. Seek for it, pray for it, believe for it. We must have it, and Heaven is waiting to bestow it."

THE HOLY SPIRIT AND THE COMMISSION FOR SERVICE

Jesus had it! The truth is that Jesus did His wonderful works and lived His beautiful life through the power of the Holy Spirit. And the help that Jesus had in living His life is also available to us. Jesus did not receive the filling of the Holy Spirit only at His baptism. Notice that He received a new baptism of the Holy Spirit every day.

Christ's Object Lessons, page 139 states: "From hours spent with God He came forth morning by morning, to bring the light of heaven to men. *Daily* He received a fresh baptism of the Holy Spirit." Emphasis supplied.

If Jesus needed that, and He was the Son of God, who else do you think might need it? And notice where He received it—within the framework of His personal relationship with His Father day by day.

You may be asking, "How long does it take?" Well, it took Paul three days, from the Damascus Road when he was converted until he received the baptism of the Holy Spirit under the ministry of Ananias. It took Peter and the other disciples three years. It took Jacob twenty years, as we have already noticed. But the counsel remains the same for all, "Seek for it, pray for it, believe for it. We must have it, and Heaven is waiting to bestow it."

Chapter 8
How to Receive the Baptism of the Holy Spirit

We have looked at the gift of the Holy Spirit in His fullness and the purpose of that gift and for whom it is available. But we would be doing an extreme disservice if we did not also spend time examining how to receive it. Let's notice several steps given in Scripture concerning how to receive the baptism of the Holy Spirit.

1. Accept Jesus as Your Only Hope of Salvation, your only hope of acceptance with God. Galatians 3:2-5, says, "This only would I learn of you, Received ye the Spirit by the works of the law, or by the hearing of faith? Are ye so foolish? having begun in the Spirit, are ye now made perfect by the flesh? Have ye suffered so many things in vain? if it be yet in vain. He therefore that ministereth to you the Spirit, and worketh miracles among you, doeth he it by the works of the law, or by the hearing of faith?"

There are two distinct issues Paul is speaking to here. First, the beginning of the Christian life. And he asks the "foolish" Galatians to stop and think how they received the Spirit in the first place. Was it by faith or by works? Then he continues, "Having begun in the Spirit, are ye now made perfect by the flesh?"

It is one thing to accept Jesus as the only hope of salvation at the beginning of the Christian life. It is another thing to continue to accept Him day by day, so that we can experience the daily outpouring of His Spirit.

One time at camp meeting, a man stopped by to talk with me

after one of the services. He was very discouraged and in doubt concerning his Christian life. He said, "I'm afraid I've gone too far. I don't think there's any hope for me. I must have committed the unpardonable sin."

I asked him to open his Bible to John 6:37 and read the verse, "Him that cometh to me I will in no wise cast out." And then I said, "What does it say in the margin?"

He said, "I don't have marginal references in my Bible."

"Well, what does it say in the white space around where the verses are printed? Is there a date on it? Does it say, like the film for your camera 'Not good after date stamped,' or perhaps, 'Good only for Smith or Jones'? "

"No."

"Then it must be good for you today." But the man had a hard time believing that. He had found it easy to believe years before, when he had first come to Christ. But there had been a lot of water under the bridge since then, and now it was harder to accept.

2. Repent of Sin. See Acts 2:37, 38. Here the apostle Peter was preaching on the day of Pentecost. He was right in the middle of his sermon, when suddenly the people interrupted by making their own altar call. It says, "When they heard this, they were pricked in their heart, and said unto Peter and to the rest of the apostles, Men and brethren, what shall we do? Then Peter said unto them, Repent, and be baptized every one of you in the name of Jesus Christ for the remission of sins, and ye shall receive the gift of the Holy Ghost."

Here is given another prerequisite for receiving the gift of the Spirit—repentance. And repentance includes what two things?—sorrow for sin and turning away from sin. But repentance is also a gift. See Acts 5:31. Therefore, sorrow for sin is a gift. And turning away from sin is a gift. Have you discovered that yet? It is only by coming into fellowship and communion with Jesus day by day, by beholding Him that we may be changed into His image, that we receive the gift of repentance.

But accepting the gift of repentance precedes receiving the gift of the Holy Spirit. Notice the following statement from *Testimonies to Ministers,* page 507, "It was by the confession and forsaking of sin, by earnest prayer and consecration of themselves to God, that the early disciples prepared for the outpouring of the Holy Spirit on the Day of Pentecost. The same work, only in greater degree, must be done now."

3. Be Baptized. This step was also given in Acts 2:37, 38. Peter instructed the people to "repent, and be baptized." Baptism symbolizes the forgiveness of sins that have been repented of. It is a public confession of Jesus Christ. And it also is the step that unites the repenting sinner to God's church.

The organized church is often criticized, and there is no arguing that there are problems within the organized church. But it was God's idea. God can work best through a group of people, instead of through separate individuals, all going in different directions. His goal for His church on earth is unity, that they may accomplish what they would have never been able to do working apart.

The church on earth is the one object upon which God bestows His supreme regard. And no matter how defective and feeble the church may appear, it is still His most powerful tool to accomplish His work.

The church can do unitedly what one person can never do. The church has sent missionaries by the thousands. How many missionaries could you send by yourself? The church has organized schools and built hospitals and clinics and printing houses. No individual could have done all that.

And there is one other factor that should be considered—the self-centeredness of God's children. Whenever He works through them in a mighty way and they become proud and lifted up because of what has been done He can no longer use them. But when He works through a group of people who subordinate self and make Christ supreme, the lines become less distinct as to exactly who it is that was used by Him to accomplish His purposes. If one person prays and He answers, that person may become proud. But if the whole church prays, who is to say which prayers were effective? And the continuing humility that can happen within the group setting enables God to continue working in ways that He might otherwise not be able to work.

God has chosen His church. Jesus prayed for it that unity might prevail. And the Holy Spirit is poured out in His fullness upon those within the church of God.

4. Become Involved in Service. Acts 5:32 says, "We are his witnesses of these things; and so is also the Holy Ghost, whom God hath given to them that obey him." Please remember the setting of this Scripture. Peter and John had been apprehended by the authorities because they had been preaching in the name of Jesus of Nazareth. After their release, they went to the company of believers and asked them to pray. Their prayer was very interesting. They didn't pray for safety or for peaceful conditions under which to work. They prayed for boldness in preaching Christ. And the place was shaken where they were.

The next day, Peter and John were back at it again, and again they were arrested. They were thrust into the common prison, but the angels came and released them. Peter and John went right back to the temple and began preaching once more. When the authorities went to the prison to find them, the guards were outside, the doors were barred, but Peter and John were gone.

In total frustration, they removed Peter and John from the temple again and began to threaten them. It was at this point in the story that Peter said, "We are his witnesses." So the obedience that was referred to was obedience in fulfilling the gospel commission, obedience in witnessing and sharing and reaching out for the sake of the gospel.

We were told a long time ago that the Holy Spirit would not be poured out upon the church until the majority of the church members became workers together with God. So the baptism of the Holy Spirit is to be given to those who are working, not to those who are inactive.

The gifts of the Spirit, which Paul lists in several places, are all service-oriented gifts. Teaching and ministry and service and healing and hospitality and all the rest of them are for the obvious purpose of reaching out to others—not simply for the enjoyment of the believer. Even the gift of tongues, which we'll look at more closely in another chapter, was given so that those who heard the good news might under-

HOW TO RECEIVE THE BAPTISM OF THE HOLY SPIRIT   65

stand what was being presented by being able to hear it in their own language.

In reality, all of the gifts of God are given that we may give again. "The gifts which the gospel offers are not to be secured by stealth or enjoyed in secret. So the Lord calls upon us for confession of His goodness. 'Ye are my witnesses, saith the Lord, that I am God.' Isaiah 43:12".—*The Desire of Ages,* p. 347.

5. Thirst for It. John 7:37-39, says, "In the last day, that great day of the feast, Jesus stood and cried, saying, if any man thirst, let him come unto me, and drink. He that believeth on me, as the scripture hath said, out of his belly shall flow rivers of living water. (But this spake he of the Spirit, which they that believe on him should receive: for the Holy Ghost was not yet given; because that Jesus was not yet glorified.)"

Don't miss that last clause. The Holy Ghost is not given until Jesus is glorified! That was true in the historical sense, but it is still true today, is it not? When Jesus is lifted up, all are drawn to Him, and the Holy Spirit can go to work.

But Jesus said, "If you're thirsty..." Are you thirsty? How do you get thirsty? One way to get thirsty is to exercise. Have you ever had it happen? Have you ever taken a long hike or climbed a mountain or mowed lawns in the summer sun? You get thirsty! And what has exercise been compared to in the Christian life? It is a symbol of the Christian witness.

Another thing that makes you thirsty is salt. What does salt represent? The righteousness of Christ. And being in the sun makes you thirsty—reminding you of the Sun of Righteousness, who arises with healing in His wings.

To be thirsty represents recognizing a need. You need water to sustain life. No man or animal can live long without it. We may be able to live several days or even weeks without food, but without water we soon die. If you become preoccupied with other things and neglect your need for water, it won't be long before you feel the results of your neglect. And it is when you realize your need most desperately that you value the water the most. The promise is given in Isaiah 44:3: "I will pour water upon him that is thirsty, and floods upon the dry ground: I will pour my spirit upon thy seed, and my blessing upon thine offspring."

He who is most aware of his need of the Spirit of God will more than likely be the one who seeks for it most earnestly, and will thus be enabled to receive it.

6. Deliberately Ask for It. If you study all of the references to the Holy Spirit in the Bible and the spirit of prophecy, it's going to take you quite awhile! But if you do, one thing will show up again and again and again. In order to receive the Holy Spirit, we must ask for it. That's simple enough, isn't it? Just ask. Luke 11:13 says that God is willing to give His Spirit to those who ask. "If ye then, being evil, know how to give good gifts unto your children: how much more shall your heavenly Father give the Holy Spirit to them that ask him?"

A promise does no one any good until it is accepted. That's true if you're talking about offers for premiums in merchandise and advertising, and it's true if you're talking about the offer of salvation from sin. No matter how trivial or how tremendous the promise may be, no one is given what is promised unless he asks for it and receives it. And the same is true for the promise of the Spirit. We must ask.

7. Believe That You Have Received It. Mark 11:24 promises, "Therefore I say unto you, What things soever ye desire, when ye pray, believe that ye receive them, and ye shall have them."

Does this mean that we are to try to force ourselves into some kind of positive thinking? No. But we are invited to claim God's blessings when we ask according to His will. Since He has already expressed His will in regard to bestowing the gift of the Holy Spirit, we can come to Him with confidence.

We may not realize where we are exactly in the progression of the works of the Holy Spirit. We may pray for the Holy Spirit and be expecting tongues of fire and a mighty wind, and the Father may answer our prayer by sending the Holy Spirit to convict us of some sin that is preventing His work in our lives. But the promise is certain, that, as we come to Him as He has invited us to come, and as we keep coming to Him, He will complete the work in our lives which He has begun.

In conclusion, notice this paragraph from *The Desire of Ages,* page 672: "Christ has promised the gift of the Holy Spirit to His church, and the promise belongs to us as much as to the first disciples. But like every other promise, it is given on conditions. There are many who believe and profess to claim the Lord's promise; they talk *about* Christ and *about* the Holy Spirit, yet receive no benefit. They do not surrender the soul to be guided and controlled by the divine agencies. We cannot use the Holy Spirit. The Spirit is to use us. Through the Spirit God works in His people 'to will and to do of His good pleasure,' Phil. 2:13. But many will not submit to this. They want to manage themselves. This is why they do not receive the heavenly gift. Only to those who wait humbly upon God, who watch for His guidance and grace, is the Spirit given. The power of God awaits their demand and reception. This promised blessing, claimed by faith, brings all other blessings in its train. It is given according to the riches of the grace of Christ, and He is ready to supply every soul according to the capacity to receive."

Does that sound like something that ought to be available to us? The baptism of the Holy Spirit is God's greatest blessing. We need it. I need it. I want it. I want all that God has to give me for power in my life and in His service. Don't you? Thank God He has provided such a wonderful gift for the needs of His children.

Chapter 9
The Search for the Spectacular

Imagine for a moment that you have just been to the doctor, and he has told you that you have a terminal illness and have only six months to live. You come home and begin trying to figure out how to tell your family the news. You start wondering what death is really like. You worry about the finances and how your family will survive without your support. You're just plain scared.

As you sit brooding in the living-room chair, your eye falls upon an advertisement in the day's newspaper. There is to be a meeting in your town this very week. A faith healer is promising instant cures for the very disease with which you are afflicted. There is a picture of someone else who was healed and a statement from his physician that "it was a miracle."

But from what you know of the background and theology and methods of this particular faith healer, you are pretty sure there is at least a 50 percent chance that the devil is the power behind the healings. Are you ready to make your decision at this point? Do you go to the meeting and accept the risk? Or do you stay home and die within six months? In other words, would you rather die—or be healed by the devil?

We have been warned that at the very end of time, there will be a tremendous effort on the part of the enemy to deceive, if possible, the very elect. Read it in Matthew 24:23, 24. "If any man shall say unto you, Lo, here is Christ, or there; believe it not. For there shall arise false Christs, and false prophets, and shall shew great signs and wonders; insomuch that, if it were possible, they shall deceive the very elect."

Apparently the enemy is going to have prepared some deceptions for the last generation living before Jesus comes again. And these deceptions are going to be performed so cleverly, that they will almost work. He's going to try to capture the attention of God's people by signs and wonders. What an easy way to get anybody's attention! Mankind has always been tremendously impressed with the sensational. When anything happens that is out of the ordinary course of events, we sit up and take notice. Hollywood is based on that premise. Circuses and fairs and carnivals have operated on that basis for years. It seems to be part of the human fabric to be fascinated by the unusual and spectacular. And the enemy is going to make use of that trait to deceive even the elect, if it were possible.

The Bible records many instances of those who were impressed by the sensational. The disciples of Jesus were impressed. Luke 10:17-20 talks about it. They had been sent out by Jesus on a missionary journey and returned in high spirits. "The seventy returned again with joy, saying, Lord, even the devils are subject unto us through thy name." Jesus patiently turned their attention away from the spectacular and focused it on the real miracle: "Notwithstanding in this rejoice not, that the spirits are subject unto you; but rather rejoice, because your names are written in heaven."

Satan had been cast out of heaven long before. It was no big deal to find that he was still subject to the power of Jesus Christ. But for stubborn human hearts to surrender to God's control and be restored to communion with Him, *that* was something to get excited about.

But we haven't learned much from this lesson to the disciples. If we were to hear of someone being raised from the dead or healed from some disease, it would hit all the headlines. Yet the sinner who is converted doesn't even make the back page.

Consider Luke 16:20-31 containing Jesus' story of the rich man and Lazarus. The rich man is portrayed as being in torment. In the parable he is pleading that Lazarus be sent to his five brothers. "Because," he said, "if someone will come back from the dead, then they will believe." The message comes back from Abraham that they would not believe, even if someone arose from the dead.

We may be impressed momentarily by that which is flashy and sensational. But does it really change hearts? Not long after Jesus gave this parable, He raised another Lazarus to life— *Lazarus,* mind you! How could they have missed the connection? But they did not believe. And when Jesus Himself was risen from the dead, they still resisted and refused and rebelled.

Acts 8 gives the story of Simon the sorcerer. Simon had been considered rather sensational in his little circle, but when the disciples came his way, he recognized that they had an even better act than his own. He wanted to cash in on the big time, and although he apparently was converted—for a while—you find that his change of heart was only temporary.

Perhaps in some way or another each one of us has stood on the mountain with Elijah, looking for God in the wind and in the fire, almost missing the still, small voice. It's an easy thing for human beings to do. It always has been so.

We are bombarded with the sensational in everyday life. "The $64,000 Question" was a program that went off the air a long time ago because it was discovered to be a fraud. But it captivated the country for a time. My wife and I used to argue with some relatives who thought this program was the greatest thing that had ever happened. We used to argue with them about the fact that these people weren't on the air to discover genius—they were there to advertise a product. The promoters would put the contestants in a sound proof booth and fire questions at them which could only be answered by someone who had the experience of a thousand years and had a photographic memory besides! The music would crescendo, the suspense would build, and the people sitting by their television sets would be just about ready to have a nervous collapse. But it was all faked.

Another form of the spectacular with which we are confronted today is the offer of getting something for nothing. It comes in many forms and is the basis for all the sweepstakes and contests and drawings that have become popular in the advertising world. The lottery is legalized in many states, and as soon as it is available, the authorities have to try to control the people on welfare who are buying lottery tickets instead of groceries to feed their families.

I remember when I was a boy I heard that Henry Ford would give a new Ford for a certain kind of penny—a certain year and stamped at a certain mint. My father was holding public meetings, and he took offerings every night. What an unbelievable opportunity to take advantage of, when faced with such an offer. Guess who was out in the back room, going through the pennies, as soon as the offering had been collected! And guess who found the right kind of penny!

I sent it to Henry Ford, airmail. And I would lie awake at night, dreaming about my new Ford. I had the color picked out and the white sidewall tires. It was going to be a convertible. I had planned the trips I was going to take my friends along to enjoy, and I was hardly able to wait for the great day to come.

Then I got a letter back from Henry Ford. That's *all* I got back from Henry Ford. A letter of regret.

We find it hard to remember that according to Scriptures, miracles or wonders are no proof of the power of God. Revelation 16:14 speaks of the spirits of devils working miracles. It doesn't say they pretend to work miracles. There is a lot of false advertising when it comes to the spectacular, but not all of the advertising is false. Let's never forget that the devil is able to work miracles. The Scripture is clear on that. We know about Pharoah and his magicians' rods in the ancient Egyptian court. They matched the miracles Moses performed, at least up to a certain point.

We are familiar with the story of Job and his boils. Do you recall who was responsible for the boils? And if the enemy can bring boils, perhaps he could have taken them away by removing whatever it was that caused the boils in the first place. It is possible by such means to make it appear that a miracle has happened.

Sometimes we praise the doctor after a successful surgery. But is the doctor able to heal the patient? They may be able to cooperate with nature by removing the cause of some problem, but that is about all they can do. Doctors may be able to sew up an incision, but the miracle takes place after that, as the wound is healing.

Let's not forget that before Jesus comes there are going to be some pretty spectacular things done under the power of the Holy Spirit. We wouldn't want to throw out all of the supernatural manifestations, automatically assuming they are from the devil. We have been promised the outpouring of the Spirit of God, the restoration of the gifts of the Spirit in their fullness in the church. But the point we want to make here is this: *Never judge truth by the spectacular!* It is never sufficient to determine whether a thing is from God or the devil on the basis of the spectacular.

We have used a lot of rationalizations for not having the full power of the Holy Spirit manifest in the church today. For instance, someone goes to Japan and learns the language and passes his medical boards in one year. We say, That's the gift of tongues. No, it isn't! We point to our hospitals and Christian doctors and their skill and talent, and say, That's the gift of healing. No it's not! Let's not sell the power of God short just because we are not experiencing it in its fullness.

There is a great burden today on the part of Christian people everywhere to experience more of the blessings and gifts of the Holy Spirit and all that goes with it. And isn't this a legitimate desire? Is there anything wrong with wanting all of the gifts that God wants to give us? Of course not. But as the search for the spectacular continues, the question is: How are we to decide if it is of God or not? That is an extremely important question.

As there are manifestations of a surpernatural character seen in various places, the temptation is to go searching for something spectacular. There are those who are going to look for more of the power of God than they have known before—and they are going for reasons far less pressing than were discussed at the beginning of this chapter, in describing someone who has only six months to live.

If you go to some of these gatherings, you can expect to find the following things:

1. You will find there an undeniable presence or power that senses cannot deny.

2. You will see the miraculous. You will see and experience that which cannot be explained by human reasoning.

3. You will find great emphasis on the Bible and on Jesus.

4. You will find a great emphasis upon love as our great need and upon the happiness and joy that come when we love one another.

5. You will find what may appear to be a more exalted system of religion, a deeper experience of faith, or deeper insight into spiritual truths.

6. And finally, you will find people whose lives have been changed.

Do you see anything wrong with that list of criteria? If you find all of these things, is it proof that the work is of God, that the spirit is the Holy Spirit, and that there is truth instead of deception?

I would like to point you to something that has been given as a special gift to the church. We can be thankful for the insights into the details of the final movements in the great controversy between Christ and Satan. Notice the following descriptions of *spiritualism* and compare them to the above list.

1. On finding an undeniable presence or power that your senses cannot deny: Satan "will present his temptations to men in a manner to pervert the senses of all who are not shielded by divine power."—*The Great Controversy,* p. 554.

2. On seeing the miraculous: "Miracles will be wrought, the sick will be healed, and many undeniable wonders will be performed."—*Ibid.,* p. 558.

3. Concerning the emphasis on the Bible and Jesus: "As the spirits will profess faith in the Bible, . . . their work will be accepted as a manifestation of divine power." "While it [spiritualism] formerly denounced Christ and the Bible, it now *professes* to accept both."—*Ibid.,* pp. 588, 558. Emphasis supplied.

4. Great emphasis on love: "Love is dwelt upon as the chief attribute of God." The enemy "appeals to the reason by the presentation of elevating themes; he delights the fancy with enrapturing scenes; and he enlists the affections by his

THE SEARCH FOR THE SPECTACULAR 75

eloquent portrayals of love and charity."—*Ibid.*, pp. 558, 554.

5. More exalted system of religion: Satan professes "to present a new and more exalted system of religious faith."—*Ibid.*, p. 589.

6. What about changed lives? "Before the final visitation of God's judgments upon the earth there will be among the people of the Lord such a revival of primitive godliness as has not been witnessed since apostolic times. . . . The enemy of souls desires to hinder this work, and before the time for such a movement shall come, he will endeavor to prevent it by introducing a counterfeit. In those churches which he can bring under his deceptive power he will make it appear that God's special blessing is poured out; there will be manifest what is thought to be great religious interest. Multitudes will exult that God is working marvelously for them, when the work is that of another spirit. Under a religious guise, Satan will seek to extend his influence over the Christian world."—*Ibid.*, p. 464.

Here is another statement on this issue: "The tempter often works most successfully through those who are least suspected of being under his control. . . . Many a man of cultured intellect and pleasant manners, who would not stoop to what is commonly regarded as an immoral act, is but a polished instrument in the hands of Satan."—*Ibid.*, p. 509.

The devil doesn't put everybody in the gutter. He'll make use of some people whose lives appear to be changed—the good, the moral, the ethical, the kind and loving. Let me ask you another question. If the devil got a person on drugs, don't you suppose he would have the power to withdraw those temptations, allowing the addict to gain the victory over drugs? Isn't this possible? So, even a changed life does not necessarily prove the power of God.

When you compare these points, you come to this inevitable question: If we cannot decide truth on the basis of any of the above conditions, then on what basis can we decide?

Well, one test is the test of Scriptures. Note: "Antichrist is to perform his marvelous works in our sight. So closely will the counterfeit resemble the true, that it will be impossible to distinguish between them except by the Holy Scriptures. By their testimony every statement and every miracle must be tested."— *The Spirit of Prophecy,* vol. 4, p. 411.

Notice another test is found in the book *Evangelism,* page 599. "Through a lack of faith, many who seek to obey the commandments of God have little peace and joy. . . . Many feel a lack in their experience; they desire something which they have not; and thus some are led to attend holiness meetings, and are charmed with the sentiments of those who break the law of God."

So if I don't have a one-to-one experience with Jesus, then trying to obey the commandments of God is not going to bring me peace and joy. I will still be looking for something that's missing in my life.

So here are two tests by which we can determine which is false and which is genuine. The first is intellectual—compare the teaching with the Word of God and the law of God. The second is experiential—have such a close relationship with God that He will be able to flash His signals to you personally, to warn you away from error and deception.

This is not in any way intended to judge the *people* who are involved in these false religious revivals. Let's consider two possibilities: (1) One person may know all about the law of God and the commandments, but lacks a deep personal experience with Christ. (2) Another may not yet accept all of the truth about God's law, but does seem to have a deep experience with Jesus. Now which of these two would be prepared for the outpouring of the Holy Spirit? Which of these two could expect to have the ultimate bestowal of the spiritual gifts and manifestations.?

The answer is, neither one! We could not expect to find the Holy Spirit in His ultimate manifestations in a group of people who are not keeping all of the commandments, nor could we expect it in a group who do not have the personal experience of accepting the righteousness of Christ. The Spirit will be poured out only upon a group that has both.

"There is a work to be done for this time in fitting a people to stand in the day of trouble, and all must act their part in this work. They must be clothed with the righteousness of Christ, and be so fortified by the truth, that the delusions of Satan shall not be accepted by them as genuine manifestations of the power of God."—*Review and Herald,* December 24, 1889.

For those who are seeking to know God and His truth, there is promise of protection from being deceived by the enemy. We can take courage when we read paragraphs, such as this one, from *The Great Controversy,* p. 560:

"Those who are earnestly seeking a knowledge of the truth and are striving to purify their souls through obedience, thus doing what they can to prepare for the conflict, will find, in the God of truth, a sure defense. 'Because thou hast kept the word of My patience, I will also keep thee' [Revelation 3:10], is the Saviour's promise. He would sooner send every angel out of heaven to protect His people than leave one soul that trusts in Him to be overcome by Satan."

There are exciting times ahead, for as surely as there is a counterfeit, there is a true. Otherwise the counterfeit would be of no value. As we see the last desperate attempts of the enemy to deceive and destroy, we can look up and lift up our heads, for our redemption draws nigh. All that we long for, in the spectacular power of God, in miracles performed, in greater involvement with the Bible and with Jesus, in love and joy and happiness and spiritual insights that go deep—all we can hope for, and more besides, will be given by the Holy Spirit as we continue to walk with Him.

Chapter 10
The Gift of Tongues

Have you heard the story of Griffith Jones? He became a Seventh-day Adventist in 1893 and had a burning desire to take the gospel to the inhabitants of the East Indies and the South Sea Islands.

But the church leaders wouldn't let him go. They said, "You're too old."

Jones was a "rebel." He decided to go anyway! And obviously he was being led by the Spirit. He hitchhiked his way, bummed his way alone aboard a freighter bound for the South Seas.

Under cover of darkness, they let him out one night off the shores of one of the cannibal islands. He contrived to secure a little boat in which to ride to shore, and he arrived on the beach with this burning desire to take the gospel to the heathen. And then something wonderful happened!

The minute his feet touched the shore, he knew their language. The next morning when the cannibals discovered him, it could have meant disaster—with "Captain Jonesie" for dinner. But when he began to talk to them in their own language, they were impressed. They listened just long enough to hear about the God of love. It touched their hearts. And the work was started in the South Sea Islands.

We are going to see a lot more of this sort of thing before the history of this earth is finished, for there is a genuine manifestation of the gift of tongues.

The gift of tongues is listed by Paul as being among the gifts of the Spirit. Let's look at all of the spiritual gifts to begin with and then focus on the one that seems to be the most misunderstood in the Christian world today. First of all, Ephesians 4, beginning with verse 8: "When he [Jesus] ascended up on high, he led captivity captive, and gave gifts unto men." Verses 11 and 12: "He gave some, apostles; and some, prophets; and some, evangelists; and some, pastors and teachers; for the perfecting of the saints, for the work of the ministry, for the edifying of the body of Christ."

Already we hear two things about spiritual gifts. *Some* people are given one gift, and *some* another. And the major purpose is for the edifying of the body of Christ.

As long as we are in Ephesians 4, notice one other verse, verse 23: "Be renewed in the spirit of your mind." God works through the mind, and we'll talk more about that a little later.

Now go to 1 Corinthians 12, where Paul begins his treatment of the subject of spiritual gifts. This continues right on through chapter 14. Here Paul starts right out by saying, "Now concerning spiritual gifts, brethren, I would not have you ignorant." Then there follows a description of how the Holy Spirit brings the gifts through different operations, and in verses 7 through 10 some of the gifts of the Spirit are listed. "The manifestation of the Spirit is given to every man to profit withal. For to one is given by the Spirit the word of wisdom; to another the word of knowledge by the same Spirit; to another faith by the same Spirit; to another the gifts of healing by the same Spirit; to another the working of miracles; to another prophecy; to another discerning of spirits; to another divers kinds of tongues; to another the interpretation of tongues."

Then Paul proceeds to point out in verse 11 that the Spirit does this "as *he* will." And verse 18: "As it hath pleased him [God]." It is according to His initiative, His choice, His will. Then there is a summary in the last chapter, beginning with verse 28, where it lists again some of the gifts of the Spirit. "God hath set some in the church, first apostles, secondarily prophets, thirdly teachers, after that miracles, then gifts of healings, helps, governments, diversities of tongues. Are all apostles? are all prophets? are all teachers? are all workers of miracles? Have all the gifts of healing? do all speak with tongues? do all interpret?" The unspoken answer to each one of these questions is No. Does everybody have the same gift? No.

Now in the Neo-Pentecostal movement of today, which is sweeping all churches, jumping all denominational boundaries, the common denominator is speaking in tongues as an evidence of having received the baptism of the Holy Spirit. The speaking in tongues is thought to be for the purpose of private worship. A person goes to his closet, finds another power taking control, and speaks in a language that the speaker himself does not understand, but which he assumes is praise to God. And that is what we want to take a long look at to see what the Bible has to say.

To begin with, let's try the hermeneutical approach. That's a big word for looking at everything the Bible has to say on a given subject and making your interpretation of truth based on the weight of evidence. This is easy to do with this topic, because there are not a lot of references to speaking in tongues, so it doesn't take long to study everything on the subject!

But the hermeneutical approach to interpreting Scripture goes way back to the Protestant Reformation, when Martin Luther and the other Reformers insisted that the Bible was safe in the hands of the layman. Their premise was that the Bible interprets itself. This is still true today.

We have used this approach for doctrines such as the unconscious state of man in death. We don't take one isolated scripture passage, such as the rich man and Lazarus, and base our doctrine on that one text. Instead, we look at everything we can find on the subject and decide from the weight of evidence.

The first reference in the gospels to speaking in tongues was given by Jesus Himself, recorded in Mark 16:17, 18. He was telling His disciples about their future work, and He said, "These signs shall follow them that believe; In my name shall they cast out devils; they shall speak with new tongues; they shall take up serpents; and if they drink any deadly thing, it shall not hurt them; they shall lay hands on the sick, and they shall recover." So by Jesus' own words the gift of tongues was predicted.

If you go back to the original language on what these "new" tongues are, you find that it meant that the tongues were new to *them*. It is not talking about some tongue that has never been known or heard of before by anybody. It's like buying a "new" car, that is, a car that is new to you!

When these disciples were told that they would speak in new tongues, the very intent of the language indicates tongues that were already used before, but were new to them.

The next reference to the gift of tongues is in Acts 2. We won't read the whole chapter, but we will take time to notice the setting on the day of Pentecost. The disciples are preaching to the crowds: "The people listened, and they said, We hear every man in his own tongue." See verse 8. Some take the position that the disciples were *speaking* in their usual language, but the people only *heard* in their own language—which if that were the case, we might have to call it the gift of ears instead of the gift of tongues!

The Acts of the Apostles, pages 39 and 40, gives us an insight into this experience: "The Holy Spirit, assuming the form of tongues of fire, rested upon those assembled. This was an emblem of the gift then bestowed on the disciples, which enabled them to speak with fluency languages with which they had heretofore been unacquainted." "Every known tongue was represented by those assembled. This diversity of languages would have been a great hindrance to the proclamation of the gospel; God therefore in a miraculous manner supplied the deficiency of the apostles. The Holy Spirit did for them that which they could not have accomplished for themselves in a lifetime. They could now proclaim the truths of the gospel abroad, speaking with accuracy the languages of those for whom they were laboring. This miraculous gift was a strong evidence to the world that their commission bore the signet of Heaven. From this time forth the language of the disciples was pure, simple, and accurate, whether they spoke in their native tongue or in a foreign language."

The next instance of speaking in tongues is found in Acts 10. Here you almost have to read the whole chapter to get the picture. But you recall Peter had been sent by God to Cornelius.

THE GIFT OF TONGUES 83

Peter had seen his vision of the sheet filled with unclean animals, and understood that he was to minister to the Gentiles. Some people think Cornelius was a rank heathen, but if you read verse 22, it says he was a just man, and one that feared God.

When Peter arrived on the scene and began to present the truth God had sent him to reveal, Cornelius and his relatives and friends were there in the house. Verse 44: "While Peter yet spake these words, the Holy Ghost fell on all them which heard the word." Peter and his associates were astonished, because they didn't expect the Holy Ghost to be poured out on Gentiles. But verse 46 says, "They heard them speak with tongues, and magnify God." Then Peter said, "Can any man forbid water, that these should not be baptized, which have received the Holy Ghost as well as we?"

Peter and the other apostles had received the Holy Ghost manifested in tongues at Pentecost, which, as we have seen, were known languages. Now he says, "As well as we." And later back at Jerusalem, in his report to the "General Conference," he said, "As I began to speak, the Holy Ghost fell on them, as on us at the beginning." Acts 11:15. So the indication from Scripture is that this was the same manifestation that had been experienced by the disciples on the Day of Pentecost.

In Acts 19 we see again the ones we noticed earlier, who didn't even so much as know whether or not there *was* a Holy Ghost. And Paul began immediately to help them understand something further in their experience. Verses 5 and 6: "When they heard this, they were baptized in the name of the Lord Jesus. And when Paul had laid his hands upon them, the Holy Ghost came on them; and they spake with tongues, and prophesied."

There is nothing in the context here to say whether this is speaking in known languages or ecstatic utterances, but on the basis of our study so far, there would be no reason to conclude that it would be anything other than a known language.

The inspired commentary gives this help. "With deep interest and grateful, wondering joy the brethren listened to Paul's words. By faith they grasped the wonderful truth of Christ's atoning sacrifice and received Him as their Redeemer. They were then baptized in the name of Jesus, and as Paul 'laid his hands upon them,' they received also the baptism of the Holy Spirit, by which they were enabled to speak the language of other nations and to prophesy. Thus they were qualified to labor as missionaries in Ephesus and its vicinity and also to go forth to proclaim the gospel in Asia Minor."—*The Acts of the Apostles,* p. 238.

Now let's go back to the difficult chapter, 1 Corinthians 14. We have noticed four of the five references to speaking in tongues, and four out of the five so far have indicated known languages, rather than ecstatic utterances. Now we look at the chapter where some believe the best evidence for ecstatic utterances is found. But on the basis of the weight of evidence, we already have a majority vote, don't we?

There is a Greek word that means *ecstasy,* but it is not used in 1 Corinthians 14. The word that is used, *glossa* (also used in Acts 2), means nothing more than "tongue or language." But the King James translators have inserted the work *unknown.* You will notice that in the older editions, the word *unknown* is in italics, which indicates that it was added by the translators.

Now do you remember the verse we already read in Ephesians 4, about being renewed in your mind? Put with that Romans 12:2. "Be not conformed to this world: but be ye transformed by the renewing of your mind." God always works through the mind. "The mind controls the whole man. All our actions, good or bad, have their source in the mind. It is the mind that worships God."—*Fundamentals of Christian Education,* p. 426. The mind worships God, not the feelings or the emotions.

With that thought, let's go quickly through 1 Corinthians 14, noticing the key words. Verse 2, understandeth. Verse 3, edification. Verse 4, edifieth. Verse 6, by revelation, by knowledge. Verse 9, understood. Verse 11, the meaning. Verse 12, edifying. Verse 14, understanding. Verse 15, understanding. Verse 16, understandeth. Verse, 17, edified. Verse 19, understanding. Verse 20, understanding. Again and again the point is made not to do anything in the church that cannot be understood or that does not edify.

What does the word *edify* mean? It means "to instruct, to improve spiritually." The whole message of 1 Corinthians 14 is that if nobody understands what is being said, nobody is edified. Verse 2: "He that speaketh in an unknown tongue speaketh not unto men, but unto God: for no man understandeth him." Verse 9: "Except ye utter by the tongue words easy to be understood, how shall it be known what is spoken? for ye shall speak into the air." Verse 11: "Therefore if I know not the meaning of the voice, I shall be unto him that speaketh a barbarian, and he that speaketh shall be a barbarian unto me." Verse 19: "In the church I had rather speak five words with my understanding, that by my voice I might teach others also, than ten thousand words in the unknown tongue." And so on. Paul repeats it again and again. If no one understands what you are saying, you do not edify them or help them spiritually.

Which leads us to our next conclusion. If I were praying in private and were to pray in a language unknown to me, I wouldn't be edified either! Isn't that obvious? If I have been given the gift of speaking in a foreign language, such as Mandarin Chinese, and I speak Mandarin Chinese in an English worship service, nobody is going to be edified. If I want to pray to God in Mandarin Chinese, I should do it in the privacy of my own closet. But if I were speaking to God in a language that even I did not understand, then there would be no edification. And words spoken without understanding are useless.

In conclusion, let's remember that even the genuine manifestation of the gift of tongues is not the Spirit's greatest work. The greatest manifestation of the Holy Spirit's power is seen in human nature brought to the perfection of the character of Christ. The only purpose, therefore, in any of the supernatural working of the Spirit of God, would be to help communicate the gospel of Christ that lives may be changed. Can we join the Holy Spirit in having that as our primary goal? What a privilege we have been given to become workers together with God to that end.

Chapter 11
The Fourth Angel's Message

Are you familiar with the fourth angel's message? As a church, we have given great emphasis to the three angels' messages. Many of us were required to memorize them during grade-school days. But what about the message of the fourth angel?

It's found in Revelation 18:1-3. "After these things I saw another angel come down from heaven, having great power; and the earth was lightened with his glory. And he cried mightily with a strong voice, saying, Babylon the great is fallen, is fallen, and is become the habitation of devils, and the hold of every foul spirit, and a cage of every unclean and hateful bird. For all nations have drunk of the wine of the wrath of her fornication, and the kings of the earth have committed fornication with her, and the merchants of the earth are waxed rich through the abundance of her delicacies."

Sometimes the symbols used in the book of Revelation can make things appear more complicated than they really are. Let's go back and break it down. First of all, what is represented by the angel? It is not speaking of a single, literal angel. Rather it is describing God's work on the earth, involving all of the forces of heaven, the Holy Spirit, the angels, God's people. It is a symbol of a mighty work going on throughout the earth—with great power, great light, and great glory.

This angel is the mighty angel of revival, and his message is what we have sometimes referred to as the "loud cry," for "he cried mightily with a strong voice." One day I heard this text quoted, and the speaker asked, "What would a strong voice be?"

A little white-haired man with a hearing aid, down near the front, shouted it out. I can still hear him. He said, "A voice that could be heard!"

As we look at this loud-cry message that is to be heard all around the world, what do we find? Is the great revival brought on by a message about devils and foul spirits and a cage of unclean and hateful birds and Babylon? Perhaps the easiest way to begin to understand this message is to understand what Babylon is all about.

Where did Babylon come from in the first place? It began at the Tower of Babel. After the flood the people who turned away from God said, "We know that God has promised not to send another flood, but we are not so sure that He is big enough to keep His promise. We'd better help Him out." So they began to build a tower from earth to heaven. It was a classic example of man trying to save himself. The very origin of Babylon was trying to save one's self by one's own works.

Nebuchadnezzar was caught in the same trap. He was the king of the Neo-Babylonian Empire. In spite of the warnings God sent him, he took the glory to himself and had to learn hard lessons before he was willing to give praise and honor and glory to God, instead of taking it to himself.

"The term 'Babylon' is derived from 'Babel,' and signifies confusion. It is employed in Scripture to designate the various forms of false or apostate religion."—*The Great Controversy,* p. 381. "Nearly every false religion has been based on the same principle—that man can depend upon his own efforts for salvation."—*Patriarchs and Prophets,* p. 73. And one more from *The Desire of Ages,* pp. 35, 36: "The principle that man can save himself by his own works lay at the foundation of every heathen religion; it had now become the principle of the Jewish religion. Satan had implanted this principle. Wherever it is held, men have no barrier against sin."

So Babylon signifies trying to save yourself and worshiping yourself instead of God. We have sometimes pointed to certain other denominations as being Babylon, but do you have to be the member of a certain church in order to be guilty of self-worship? Or could this message be a warning to everybody? Would it be possible to be a victim of Babylon even while belonging to a church that warns against Babylon?

If I don't have time to spend alone with Jesus day by day, in personal faith and trust and relationship with Him, then I am trying to save myself. According to surveys, 75 to 80 percent of the members of the church do not have time to spend even five minutes a day with their Saviour. It is inevitable then, that they are trying to save themselves.

Every few years someone will rise up with a message about the Seventh-day Adventist Church becoming Babylon, and Babylon representing the church. But it takes more than individual members who are trying to save themselves to make a church or institution guilty of the sin of Babylon. We can give lip service to our need of a Saviour, and the church can doctrinally accept the righteousness of Christ in the sinner's behalf. But in order to be free from Babylon myself, I must not only have my membership in a church—I must also be willing to admit that I cannot save myself, and then come to Jesus for salvation, on a personal basis.

What is the loud-cry message, the great revival that comes under the message of this fourth angel? It is the revival of the good news that there is only one hope of salvation, and that is to trust in the righteousness of Christ. And this is the message that belts the earth with power and great glory just before Jesus comes again.

With that in mind, let's look at the beginning, the content, and the end of this mighty angel's message. If you have studied the history of this church, you know that around 1888 there was a great emphasis upon Jesus as our only hope of salvation. By 1892, as the message had gained in momentum in spite of opposition, we find the following written to the church, in the *Review and Herald* of November 22, 1892. "The time of test is just upon us, for the loud cry of the third angel has already begun in the revelation of the righteousness of Christ, the sin-pardoning Redeemer." This revelation was the beginning of the light of the angel whose glory shall fill the whole earth—the angel of Revelation 18.

A week later, November 29, 1892, the *Review* carried this statement: "A work is to be accomplished in the earth similar to that which took place at the outpouring of the holy Spirit in the days of the early disciples, when they preached Jesus and him crucified. Many will be converted in a day; for the message will go with power." So the righteousness of Christ, the message of the sin-pardoning Redeemer, was the beginning of the message of the fourth angel.

Now let's look at the *content* of the message. "All power is given into His [Christ's] hands, that He may dispense rich gifts unto men, imparting the priceless gift of His own righteousness to the helpless human agent. This is the message that God commanded to be given to the world. It is the third angel's message, which is to be proclaimed with a loud voice, and attended with the outpouring of His Spirit in large measure."—*Testimonies to Ministers*, p. 92. So that's the content of the revival message.

And the end of the message of this mighty angel? "The message of Christ's righteousness is to sound from one end of the earth to the other to prepare the way of the Lord. This is the glory of God, which closes the work of the third angel."—*Testimonies*, vol. 6, p. 19.

So the beginning, the content, and the conclusion of the message all center around righteousness by faith in Jesus Christ alone. And whenever you hear an emphasis upon that message, you can take courage and lift up your head and rejoice, because your redemption draws nigh.

You may have realized in the above quotations that the message of this fourth angel and the message of the three angels and the third angel's message are referred to almost interchangeably. That is because the fourth angel does not bring a new message, but simply brings a new, or renewed, emphasis upon the message already brought by the three angels of Revelation 14. But the intent of the three angels' message of Revelation 14 has been lost sight of for a time.

You might be painfully aware that God's people have wandered in the wilderness for many years, just as did ancient Israel. The time of wilderness wandering has been characterized by an absence of emphasis upon Christ as our only hope of

THE FOURTH ANGEL'S MESSAGE 91

righteousness. But the good news is that we don't have to stay in the wilderness forever. The time will come when Psalm 126 will be fulfilled. "When the Lord turned again the captivity of Zion, we were like them that dream. Then was our mouth filled with laughter, and our tongue with singing: then said they among the heathen, The Lord hath done great things for them." Verses 1, 2. There comes a time when God's people, who have been slumbering and sleeping, wake up, as from a dream. And the waking up centers around the realization of wherein lies our only hope of salvation.

Now we have come up with some terms that are, I suppose, rather unique to our Adventist subculture, the "early" or "former rain" and the "latter" rain. Of course, these are biblical terms found in Hosea 6:3; Zechariah 10:1; and James 5:7, 8. They indicate that in God's great harvest field, you need rain to get the wheat or grain started, you need showers all along the way, and you need a good, heavy rain just before harvest. You don't have to be a farmer to realize the importance of rain.

We have called the Day of Pentecost the early rain and have looked forward to the last great outpouring of God's Spirit upon the earth as the latter rain. The latter rain, or loud cry of this fourth angel, is the message of warning against self-worship and the invitation to accept the righteousness of Christ. It starts small, but swells into a loud cry. Everybody is going to hear. And I believe it has already started.

The latter rain, as we have seen, is the final manifestation of the baptism of the Spirit. You don't have to wait for the latter rain to have the baptism of the Holy Spirit; in fact, we are told that we should *not* wait for it. But you need the same preparation for the latter rain as for the baptism of the Spirit at any time in the earth's history.

The baptism of the Spirit doesn't have any timetable on it. It has been available since Pentecost and was evidently available way back into the Old Testament as well. But the latter rain does have a timetable on it, because it is the last outpouring of the Spirit before the end.

The latter rain, the loud cry, and the finishing of God's work in the earth have a few distinguishing marks. One of the first is that God is going to take the reins into His own hands. See *Testimonies to Ministers,* p. 300. That was an expression from the horse-and-buggy days. In our day, we would probably say, God is going to take the wheel; He's going to get into the driver's seat. And when that happens, we are going to be surprised at the simple means He will use to accomplish His will.

"The message will be carried not so much by argument as by the deep conviction of the Spirit of God."—*The Great Controversy,* page 612. Sometimes we get bogged down in arguments and debates. Some preachers in the last century loved to argue and debate, and they were reprimanded for it. But this is not true of the proclamation of the message of the fourth angel.

Early Writings, page 277, tells us something else about this great revival: "Angels were sent to aid the mighty angel from heaven, and I heard voices which seemed to sound everywhere, 'Come out of her, My people....' This message seemed to be an addition to the third message."

As we have already mentioned, the message of the fourth angel is new primarily in terms of timing and emphasis, not in terms of content. The message has already been given in the three angels' messages, but for a time has been lost sight of.

We are told that the genuine manifestation of the gift of tongues will be poured out. See *Gospel Workers,* 1892 edition, pp. 383, 384. "Miracles will be wrought, the sick will be healed."—*The Great Controversy,* p. 612.

Few "great men" will be involved in this final work, for God often cannot work through individuals who possess great talent without their taking the credit for the success of the endeavor. See *Testimonies,* vol. 5, p. 80.

Man's inventions, human gimmicks and machinery will be swept aside, and God will work through the most simple means. See *Selected Messages,* bk. 2, pp. 58, 59.

I remember sitting on a hotel veranda in Luxor, Upper Egypt. We were about ready to leave after our tour with Dr. Horn, and here was one lone missionary who worked in and out among the humble huts in that land. It is one of the least advanced civilizations in the world.

One of the doctors in our group leaned forward and asked, "What do you need? We are ready to supply you with anything you need to carry on your work. Would you like a projector or screens or other equipment?"

And the missionary responded, "What we need is more prayer!" That night our train pulled out for Cairo. An executive from the railroad company was being promoted to Cairo, to a higher position. He was a great man. Many had come to wish him well. They were shouting and singing and waving. And over in the shadows stood the lone SDA missionary. As we pulled away into the darkness, I could still hear his words. "What we need is more prayer."

When the boundaries of man's authority are swept away and the Holy Spirit moves in to complete His work, we are going to realize the futility of all of our own efforts, even in doing the work of the Lord. And we will recognize with the lone missionary from Upper Egypt that the answer all along has been in more prayer and less self-effort.

Another truth about the loud-cry revival, found in the *Review and Herald* of November 19, 1908, says, "Only those who have withstood temptation in the strength of the Mighty One will be permitted to act a part in proclaiming it [the third angel's message] when it shall have swelled into the loud cry." That means I must know the power of God to pull out of Babylon and learn to depend completely upon Him before that time, doesn't it?

And finally, the warning has been given that there will be great opposition to the revival of this fourth angel. From the *Review* of May 27, 1890: "The light which will lighten the earth with its glory will be called a false light, by those who refuse to walk in its advancing glory." And in the *Review* of December 23, 1890, we read: "In the manifestation of that power which lightens the earth with the glory of God, they [those who are blinded by Satan] will see only something which in their blindness they think dangerous, something which will arouse their fears, and they will brace themselves to resist it."

In conclusion, let's look briefly at the events which are to occur between now and the time when Jesus comes again.

1. There is to be a great emphasis upon righteousness by faith in Jesus. Have you heard it?

2. This emphasis causes a shaking among God's people. The lukewarm disappear, going one way or the other, either hot or cold. This is happening all around us today.

3. The Holy Spirit and the angels begin to leave those who are not interested and double their numbers around those who are.

4. As God's people learn to seek Jesus and depend upon Him, instead of depending upon themselves, they gain the victory—victory over self-dependence, which results in victory over every sinful deed and thought.

5. Those who finally gain the victory become involved in the loud cry of the third angel, the great revival. They begin to share the good news with a power never before experienced.

6. As they go forward in the power of the latter rain, the fears of the ungodly are aroused, and persecution and times of trouble begin.

7. As the persecution mounts, the time of trouble for God's people is reached, and they wrestle with God day and night for deliverance.

8. Finally, Jesus is seen coming in the clouds of heaven, and it's time, at last, to go to a better country.

Have you ever looked up into the blue sky on a sunny afternoon and tried to imagine what it would be like to see the heavens part as a scroll when it is rolled together? And have you ever found that your imagination was unequal to the scene and felt it was almost unbelievable that it would ever really happen?

But then have you ever looked at just a small corner of the suffering and sorrow and pain and tears in this world gone wrong, and found it even more difficult to imagine that it would *not* happen?

We have been so comfortable here. We have been so content in this world of sin. We have settled for so little of the power of God in our lives. But the Holy Spirit, our best Friend, works continually to draw us away from our complacency. He works day and night to show us our sin, our need of a Saviour, and to bring us to surrender ourselves and our plans, that we may be used of Him to bring an end to the world of sin. Are you willing, today, to allow Him to work in your life? Will you seek for His power tomorrow and the day after and every day until Jesus comes and takes us with Him for eternity?